Barn Quilt Patterns

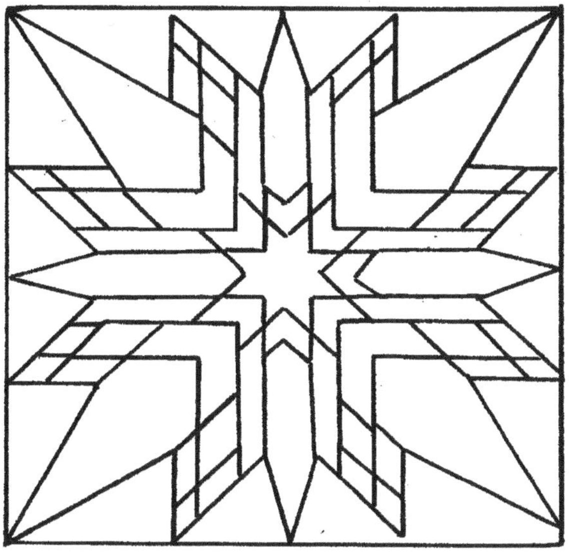

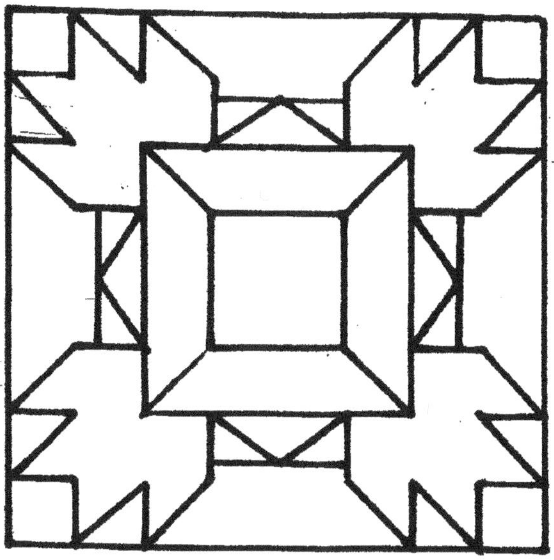

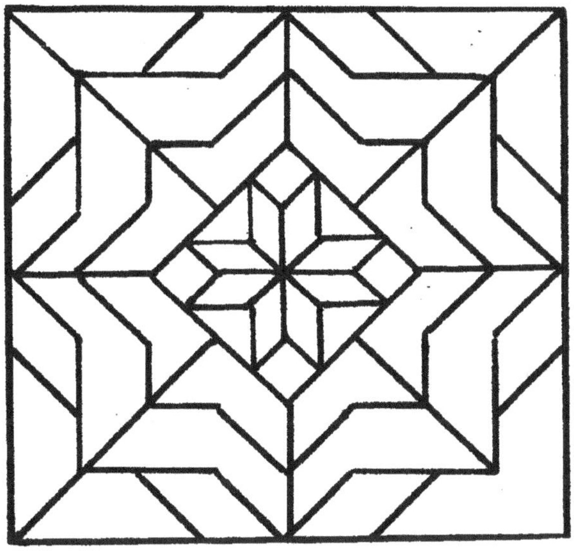

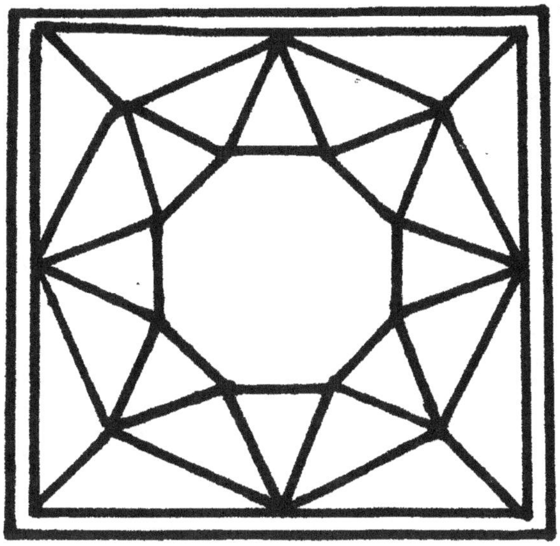

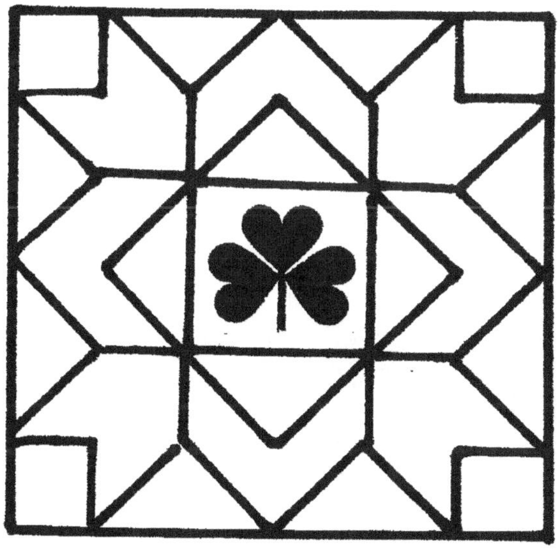

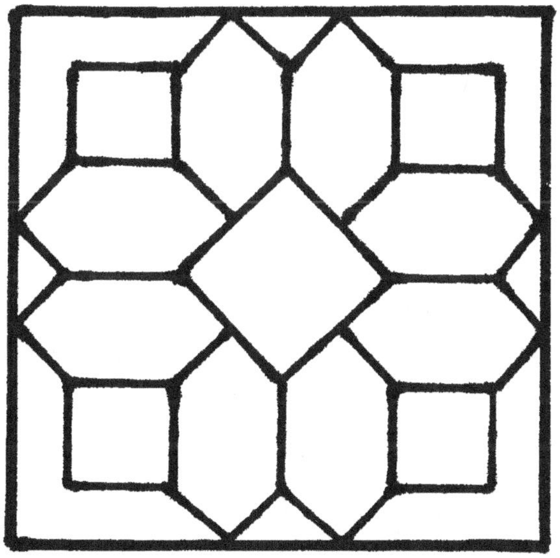

Barn Quilt Pattern Book
John H. Lettau

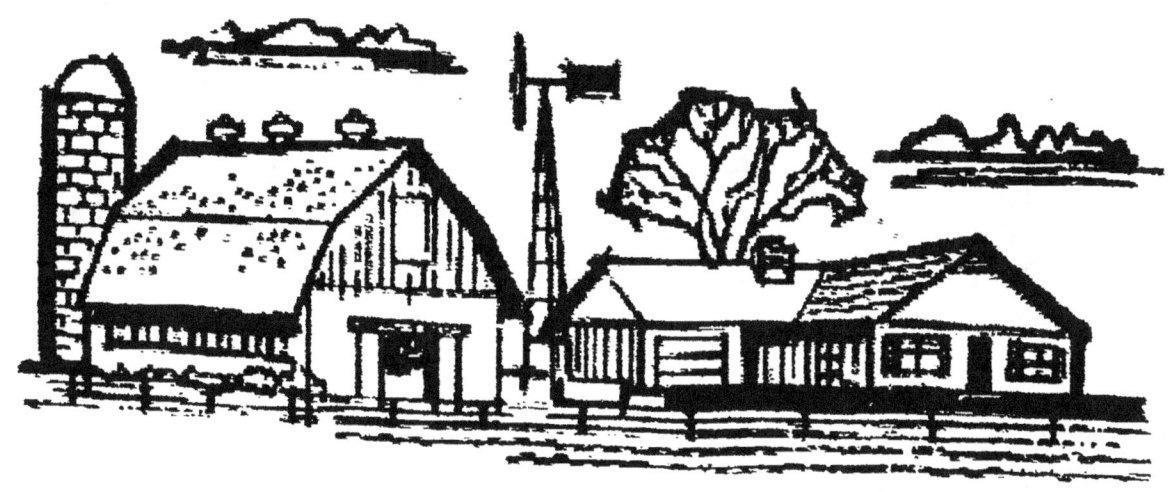

*Featuring Many Common & Unique Patterns
Around the United States & Canada*

*Usable as coloring book and/or pattttern resource for..
Quilters & Quilting Guilds*

Copyright John H. Lettau 2018

History of Barn Quilts

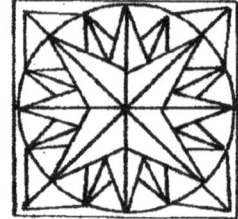 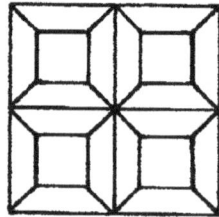 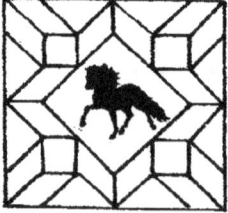 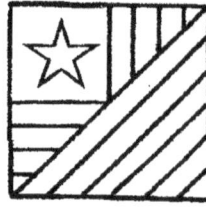 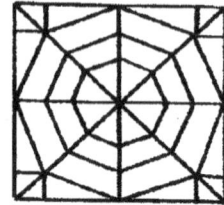

Today colorful barn quilts,"quilt blocks," can be found along many highways, rural back roads and even in towns and cities through-out America and Canada. The interest in this fast growing grass root arts movement started not many years ago in Ohio and continues to grow daily as communities, social groups and clubs see what barn quilts can do to promote tourism and the local history/heritage. Brilliant barn quilt patterns are displayed on barns, corn cribs, and other farm out-buildings through out farm country and even in towns and cities. Five examples barn quilt patterns in this book are pictured above... Mariner's Compass, Spools, Peruvian Horse, Folded Star and Homecoming. This book is an opportunity for you to create many original color design patterns for the above patterns.

Barn Quilt Projects are usually supported and organized to educate, promote and celebrate the unique agricultural heritage of an area through the visual combination of barns and quilt patterns, Farms are vital to the economic well-being of many rural communities. Handmade quilts provided warmth, beauty, and an outlet for individual artistic expression. Plus, tourism is an important part of local barn quilt projects.

Information on How Barn Quilts are Constructed

A barn quilt is made by painting a barn quilt design on two 4' by 8' sheets of 3/4 inch plywood suitable for weathering out door in all forms of weather. Prior to painting the barn quilt pattern two or three coats of primer are applied to front, back and all edges of the plywood. Next, draw the barn quilt pattern. Frog Tape (painter tape) is then applied to outline all section of the design. Two coats of each color are painted, with each coat allowed to dry overnight. After the quilt is finished it is allowed to dry and cure for two weeks before being mounted on a barn or other building.

Each quilt design is usually painted by a team of volunteers and require a willing farmer owner to donate hanging on their barn or other structure. Making these quilt squares allows volunteer groups from churches, schools, 4-H, other community service groups, and even families the opportunity to create and paint their own quilt square as a group project. The chosen square may represent a family pattern from a beloved family quilt.

Interesting Facts on Barn Quilts

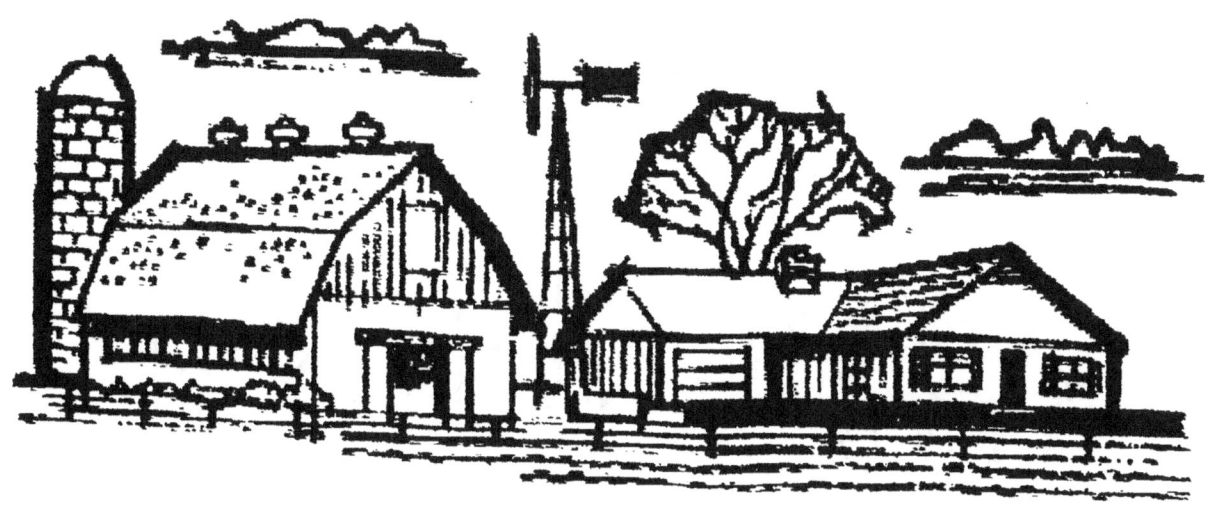

1. Common designs, such as Corn & Beans, are found in many states & rural areas.
2. The same quilt pattern will be found with a different color pattern.
3. It is not uncommon to find the same pattern with different names.
4. Some common patterns have small modification with an extra line or lines.
5. Barn quilt patterns may honor individuals, families, and/or groups.
6. Many times color selections may have a special family meaning.
7. Sometimes quilt patterns are family designed, named, and painted.
8. Some city libraries and social clubs organize senior coloring programs.
9. Some select a common pattern and just change the coloring pattern and/or name.
10. Some find a poplar pattern and change the name with a new meaning.

Typical Barn Quilt Project Objectives

1. Reflects the agricultural heritage and history of the town or region.
2. Barns or buildings are highly visible from highway or road.
3. Have buildings bring pride to the area.
4. Promotes well maintained barns and other farm or town buildings,
5. Promotes tourism for and in the area.

Objectives of Barn Quilt Coloring Books

1. Provide a relaxing activity for families and friends.
2. Help reduce tension & stress in daily life.
3. Create a fun an enjoyable activity for all age groups.
4. To bring various groups together.

Group Patterns in This Book

Patriotic Barn Quilts

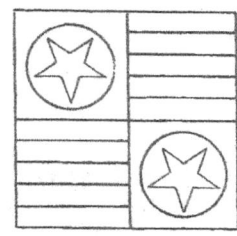 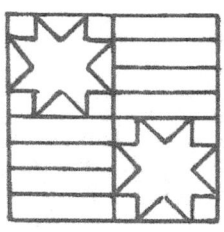 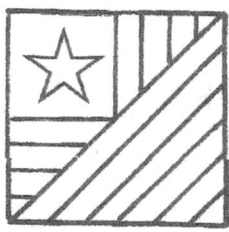 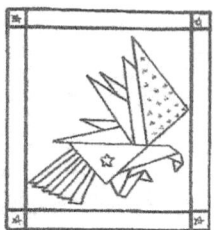

Club Barn Quilts

 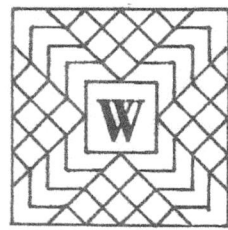 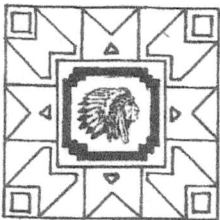 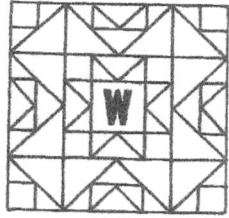

Farm Equipment

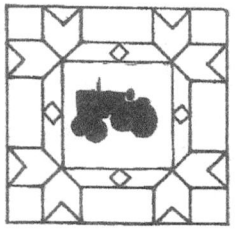 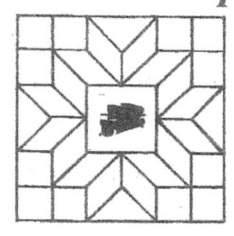 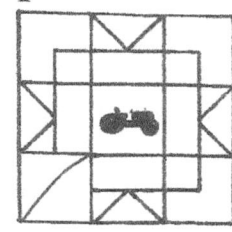 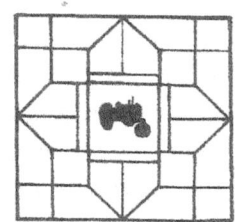

Animals

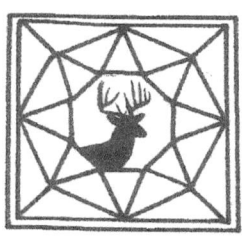 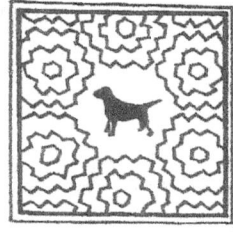 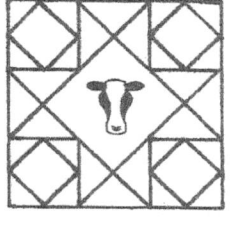

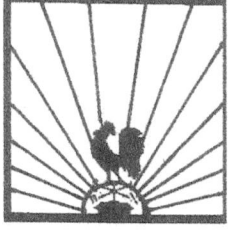 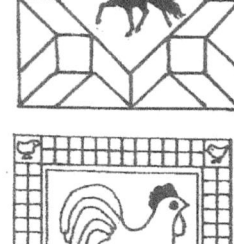 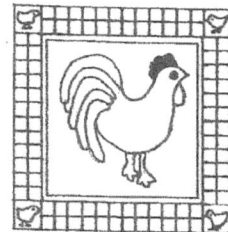 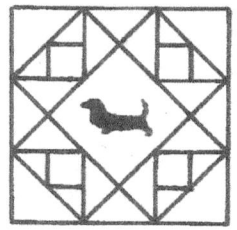 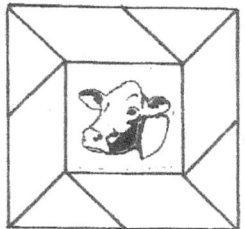

Birds

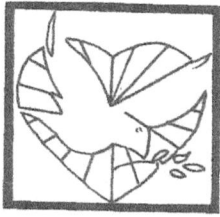 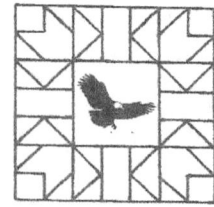 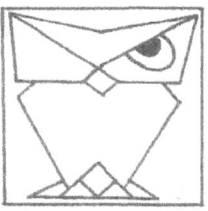 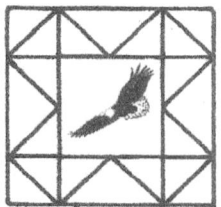

Barn Quilt Patterns

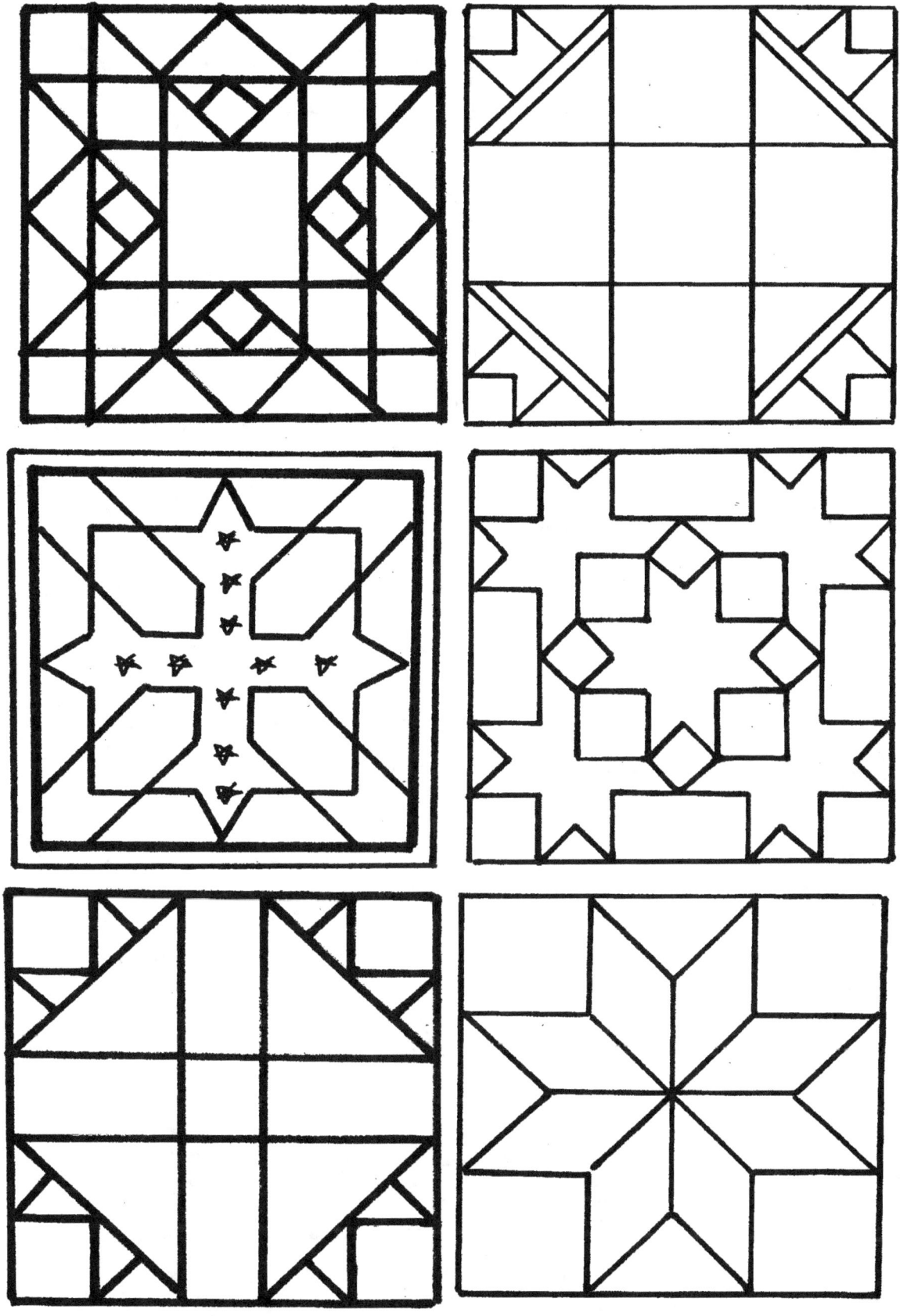

Barn Quilt Patterns

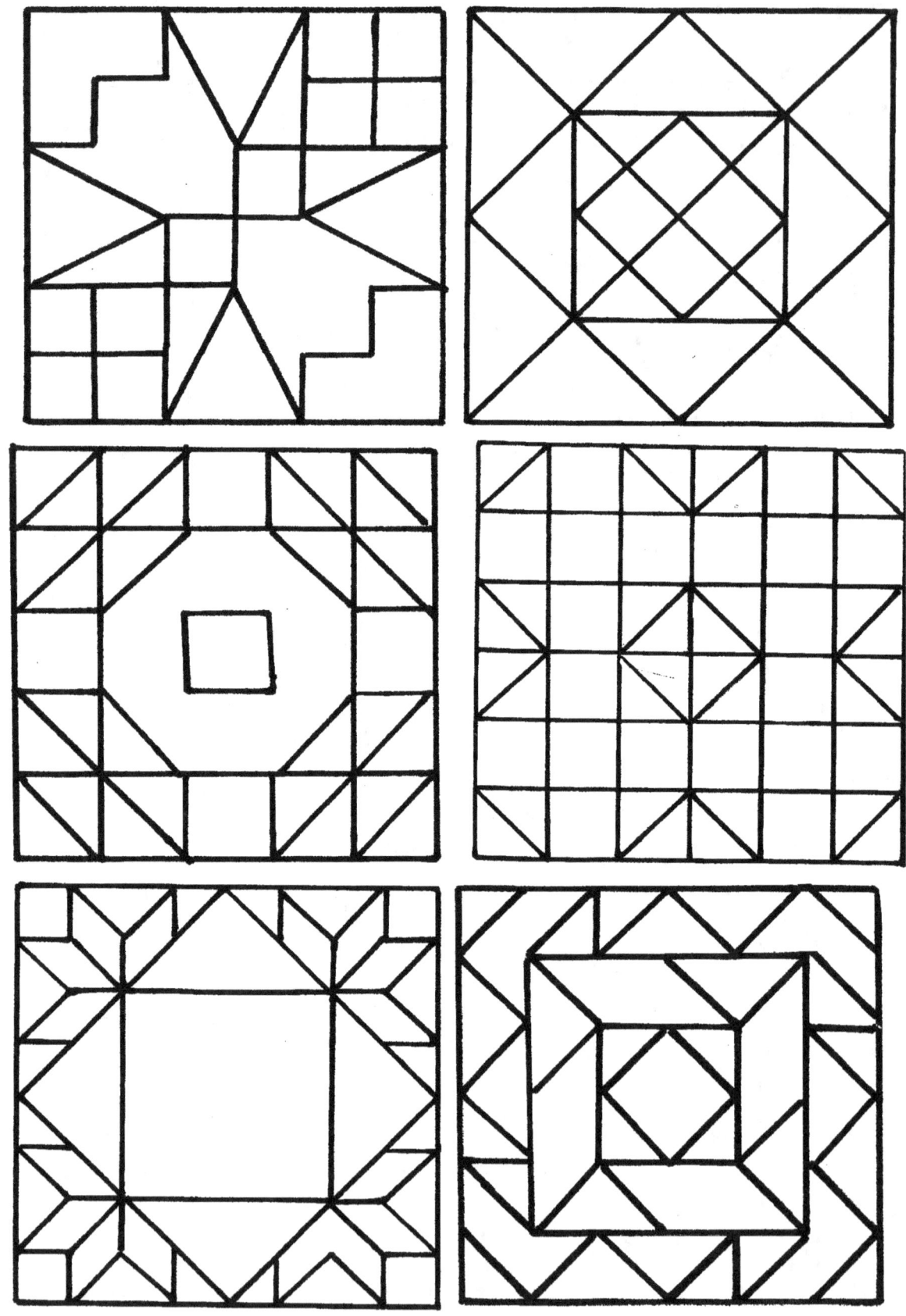

Barn Quilt Patterns

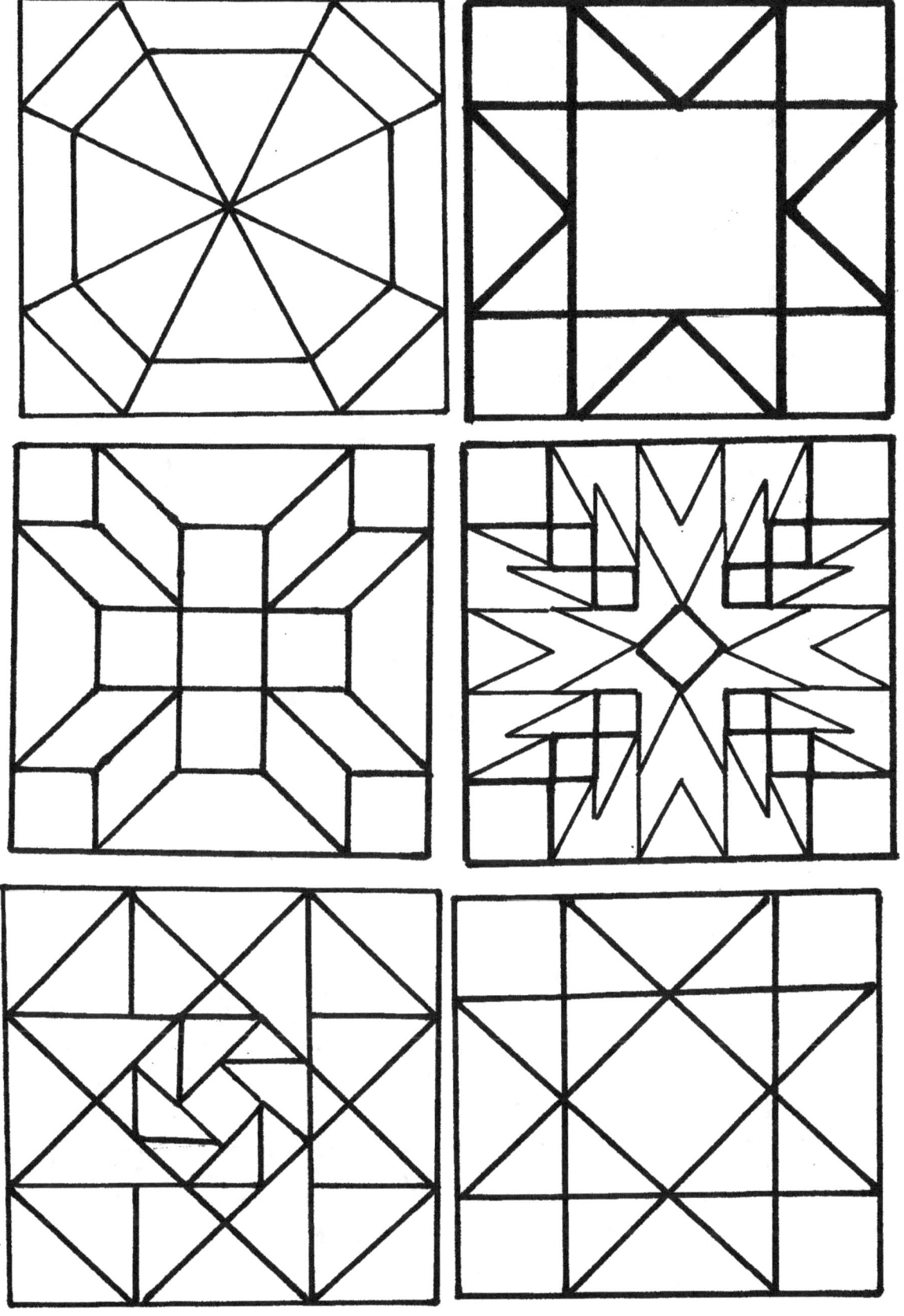

Barn Quilt Patterns

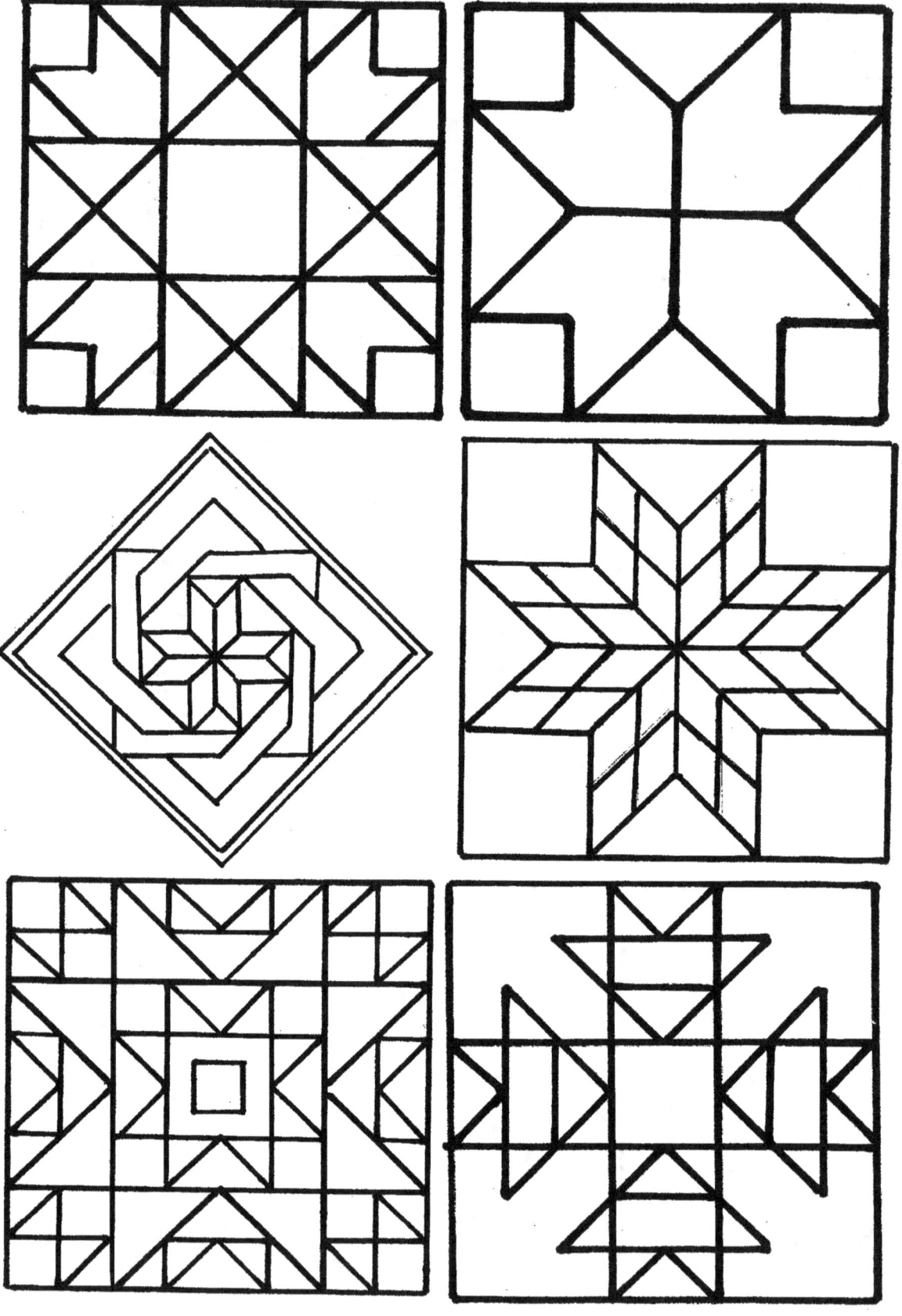

Barn Quilt Patterns

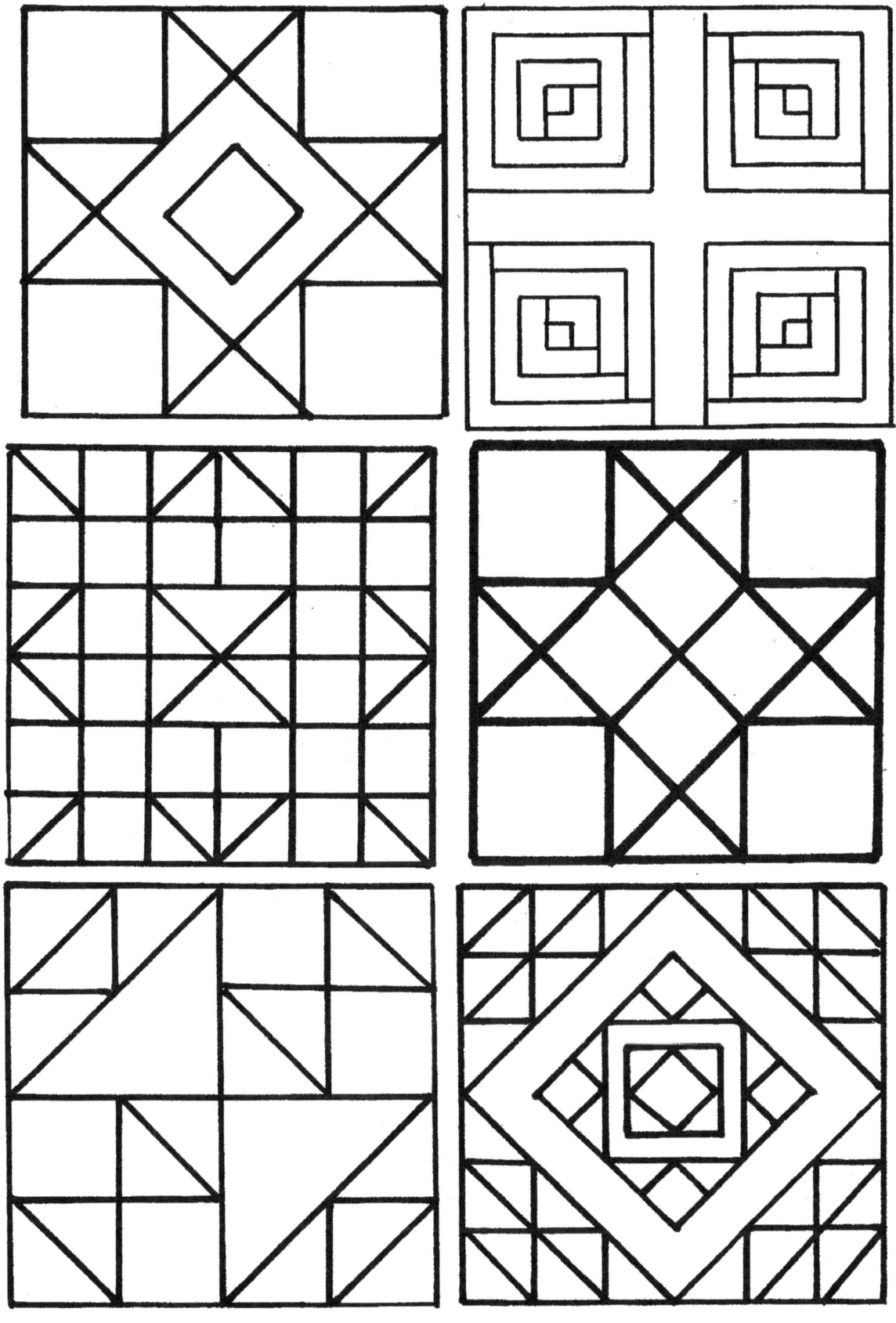

Barn Quilt Patterns

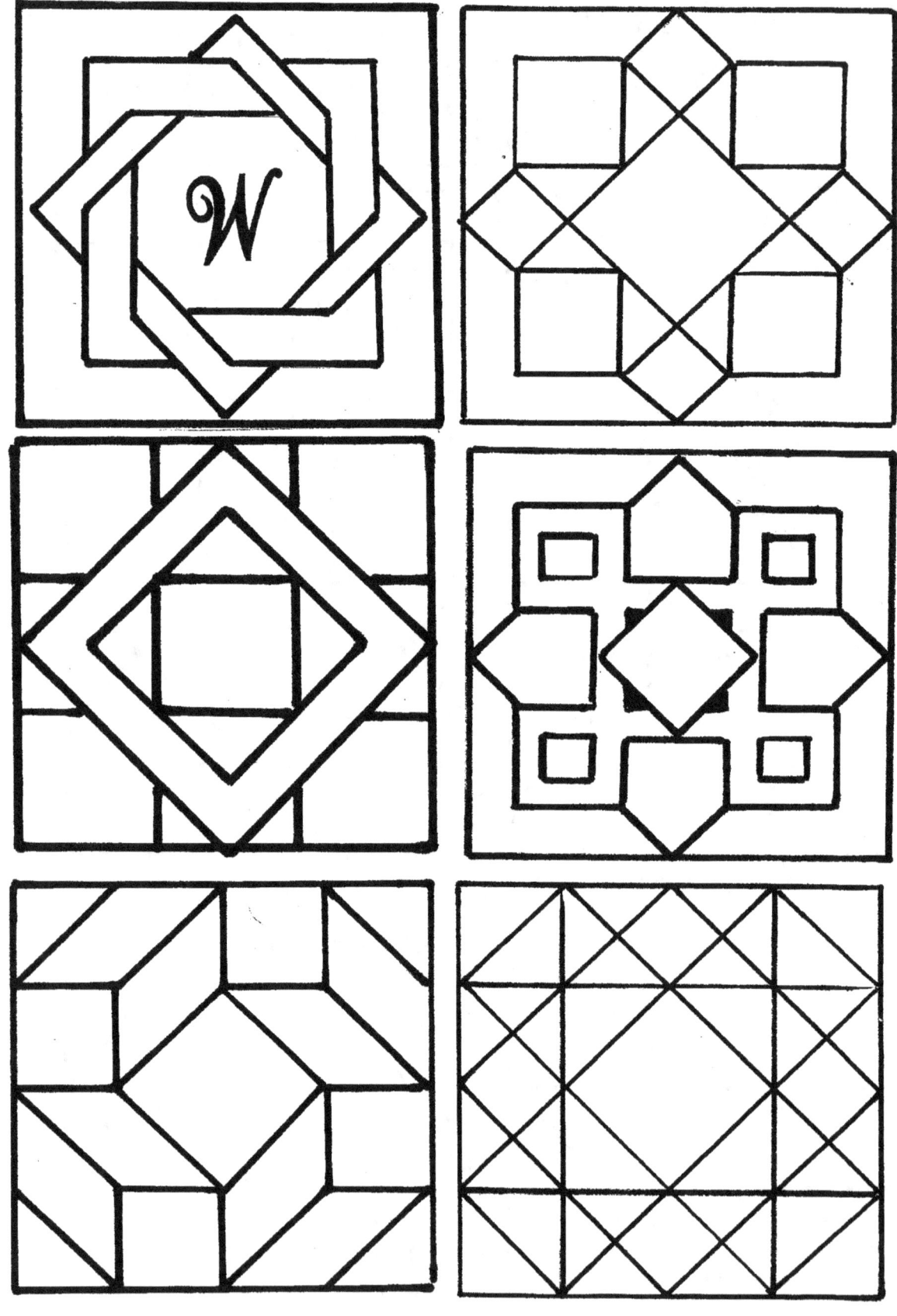

Barn Quilt Patterns

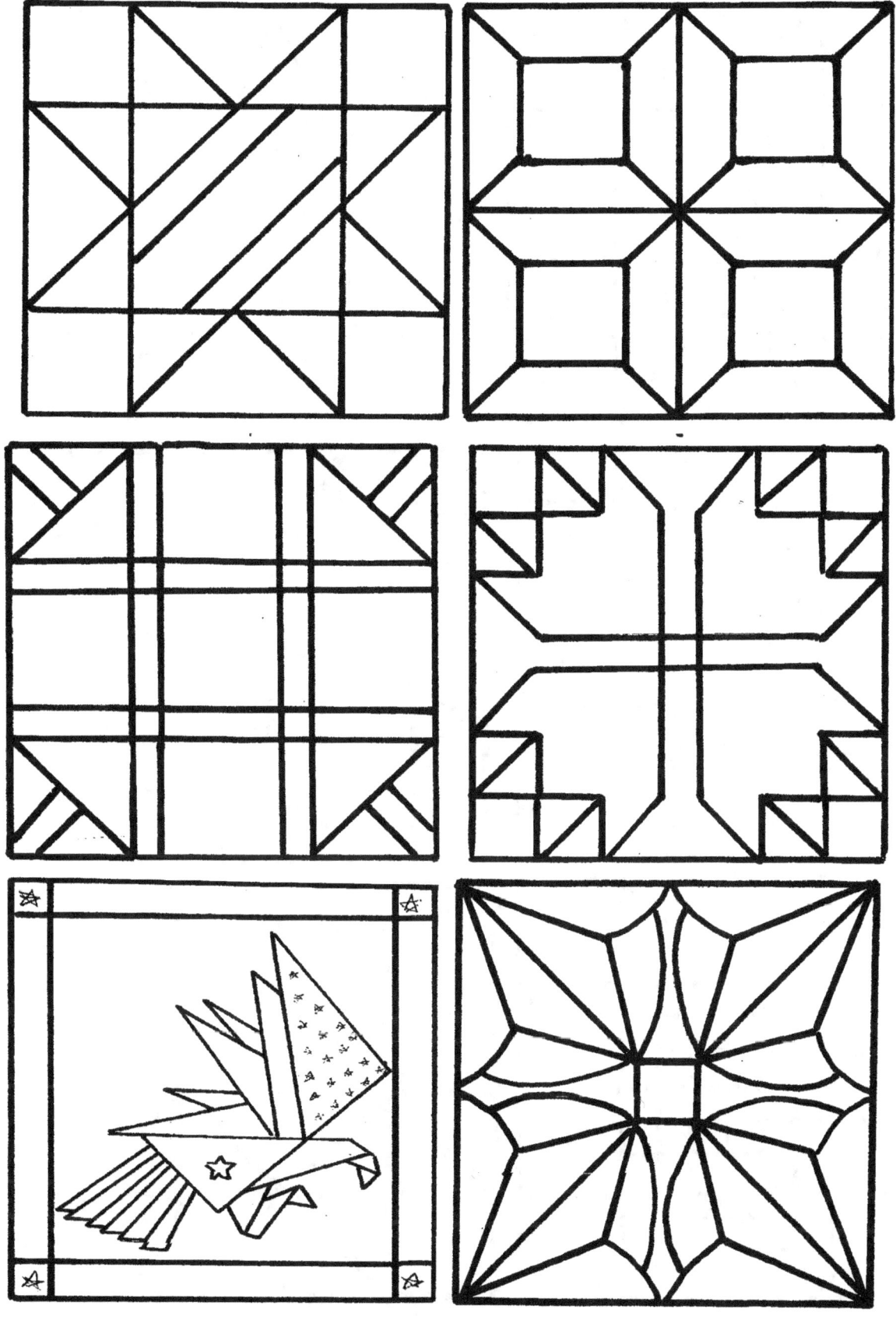

Barn Quilt Patterns

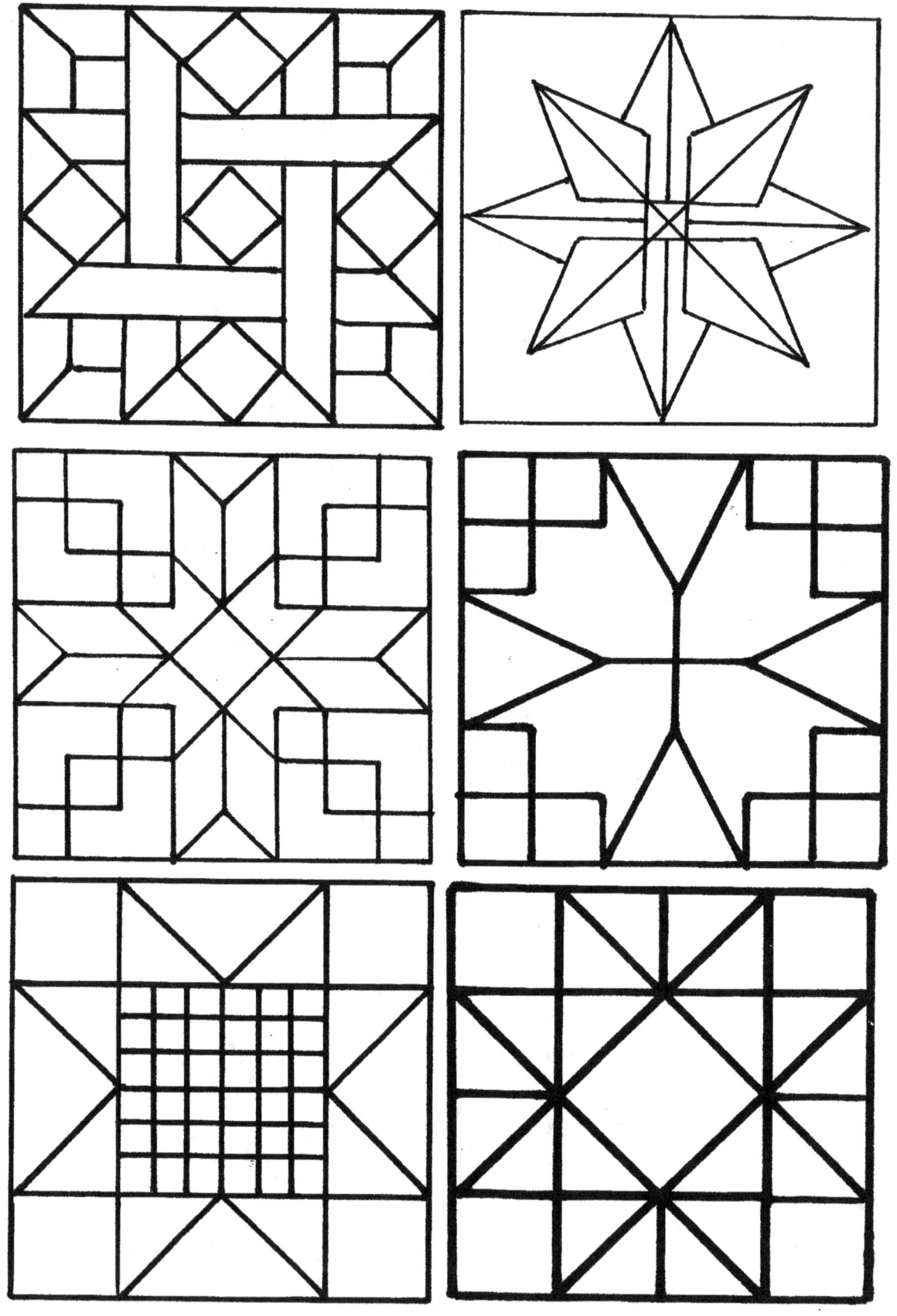

Barn Quilt Patterns

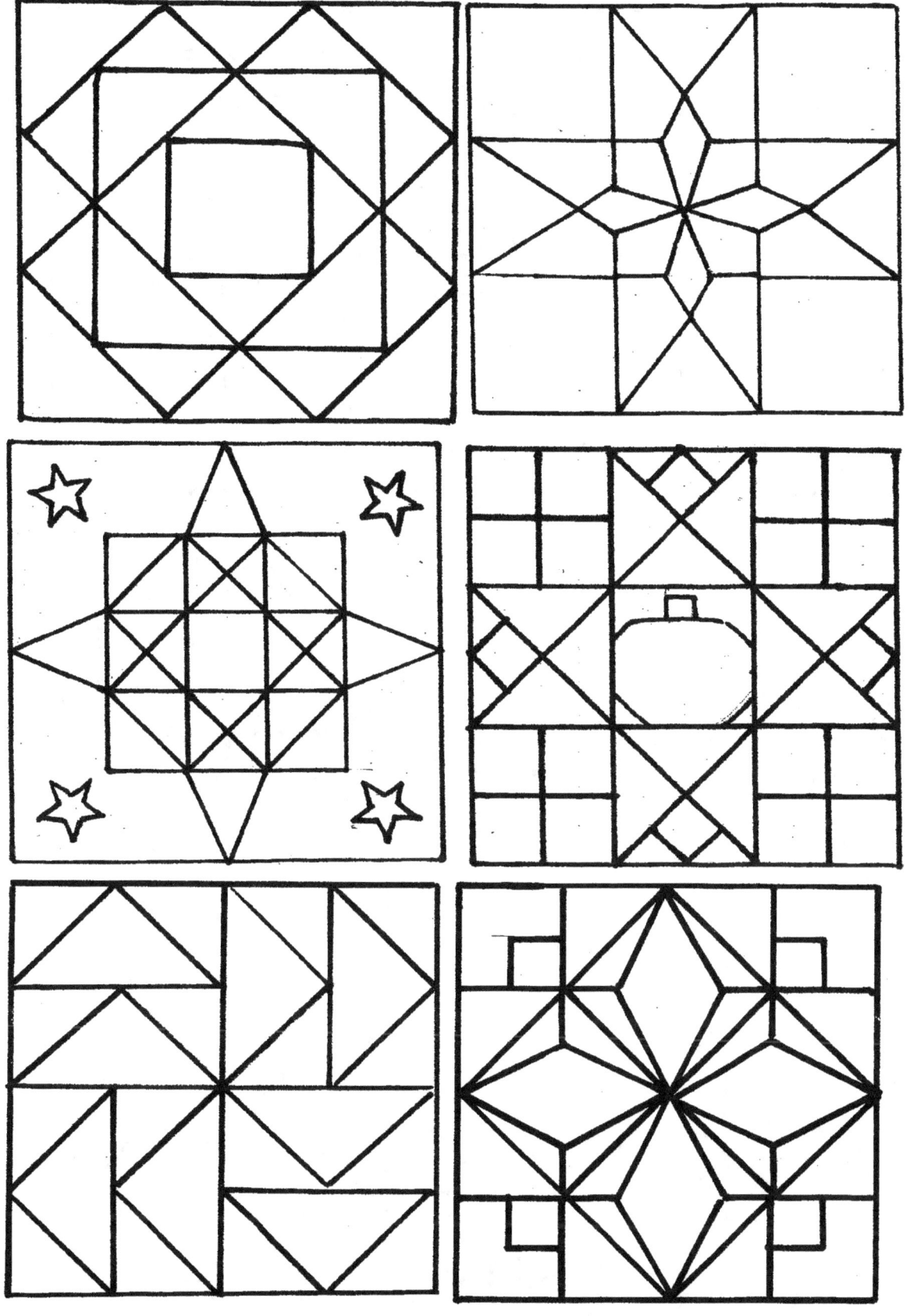

Barn Quilt Patterns

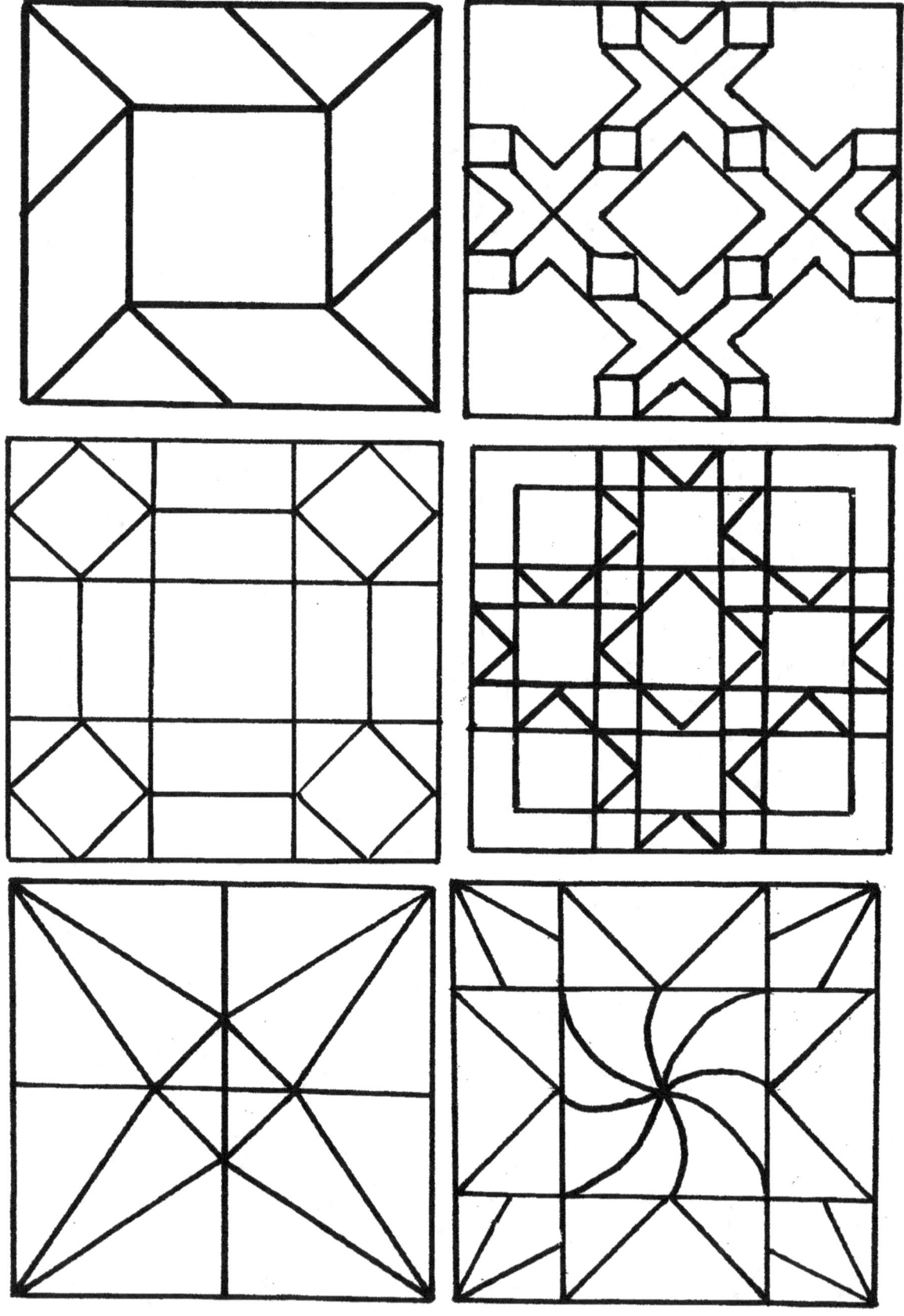

Barn Quilt Patterns

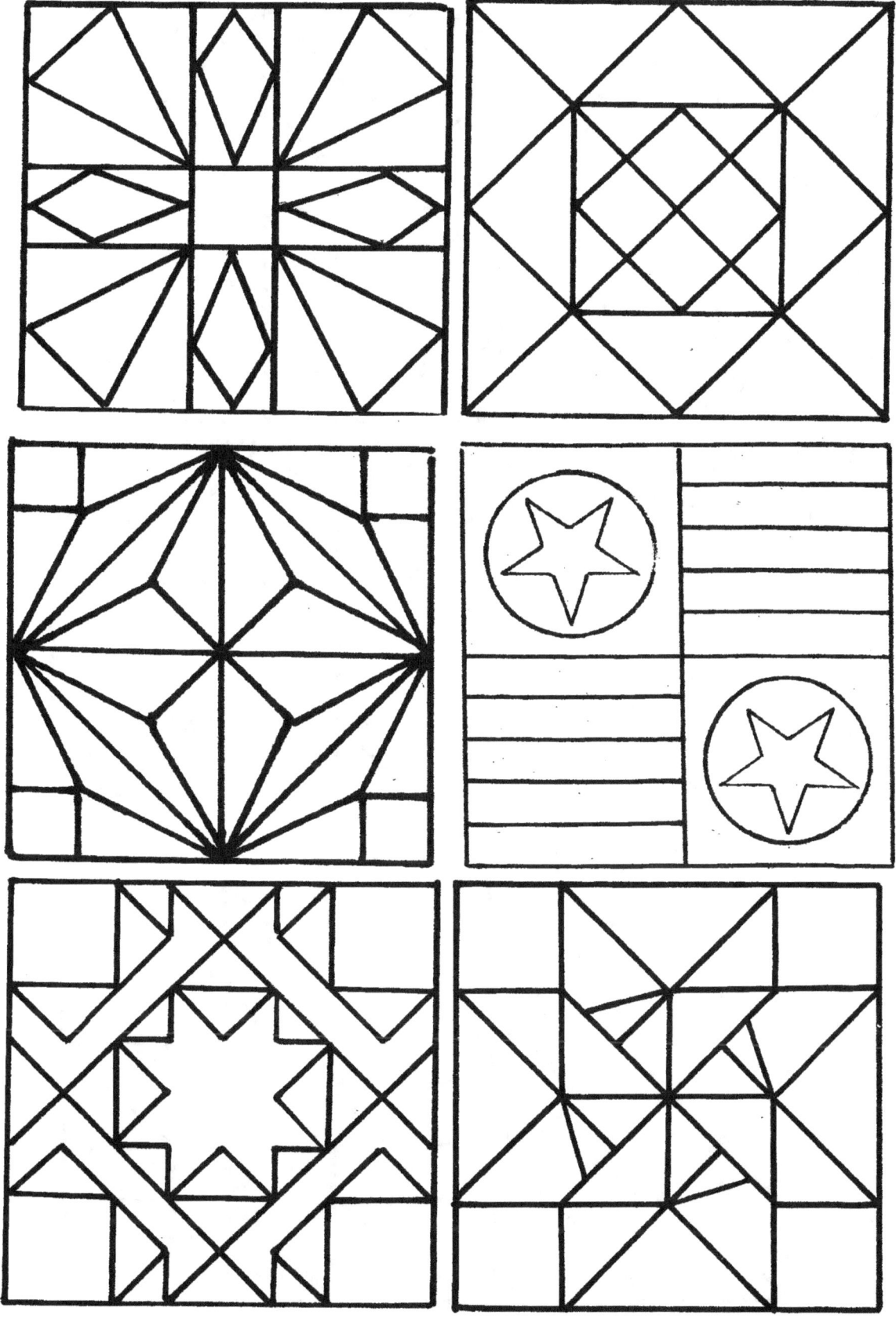

Barn Quilt Patterns

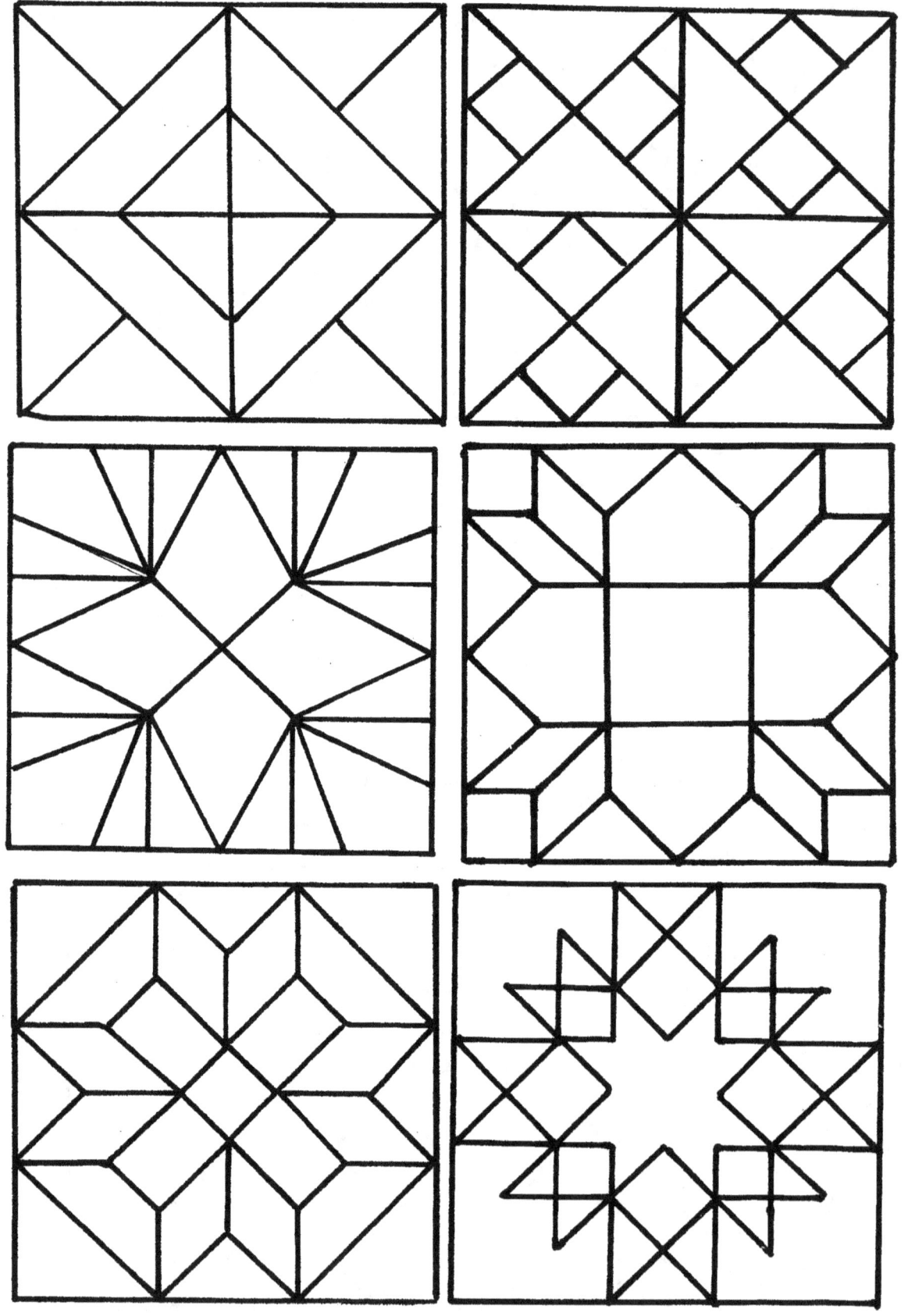

Barn Quilt Patterns

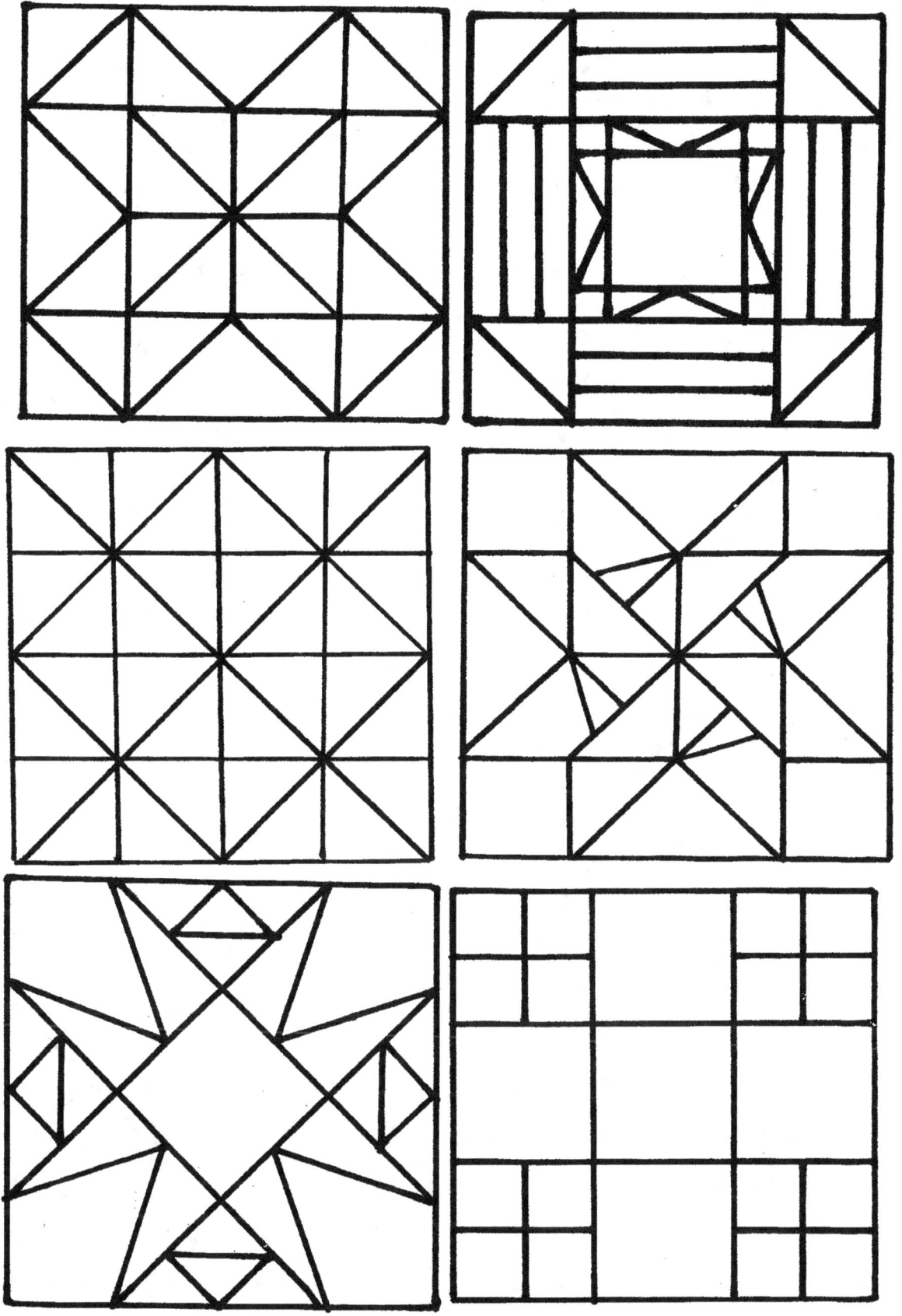

Barn Quilt Patterns

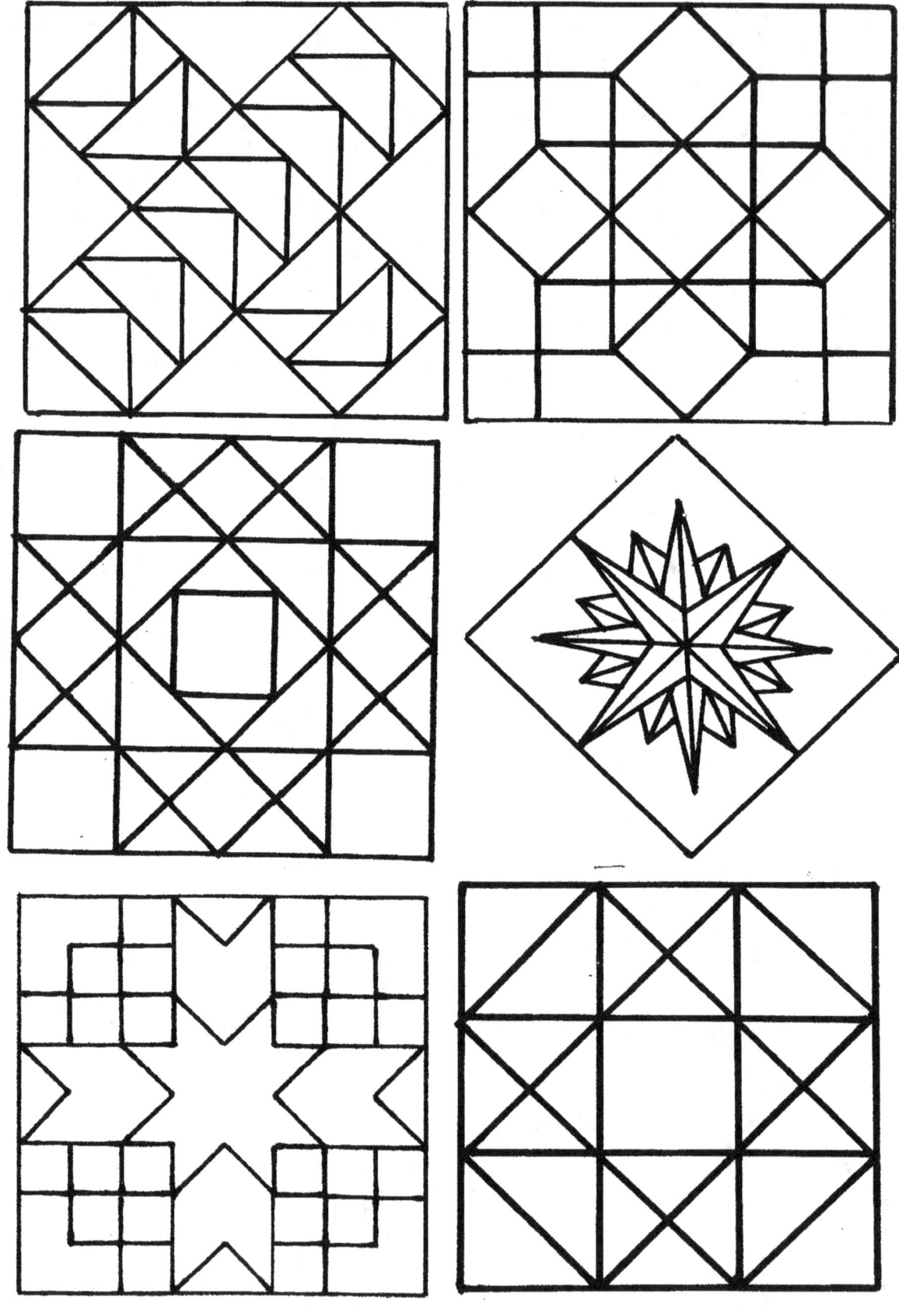

Barn Quilt Patterns

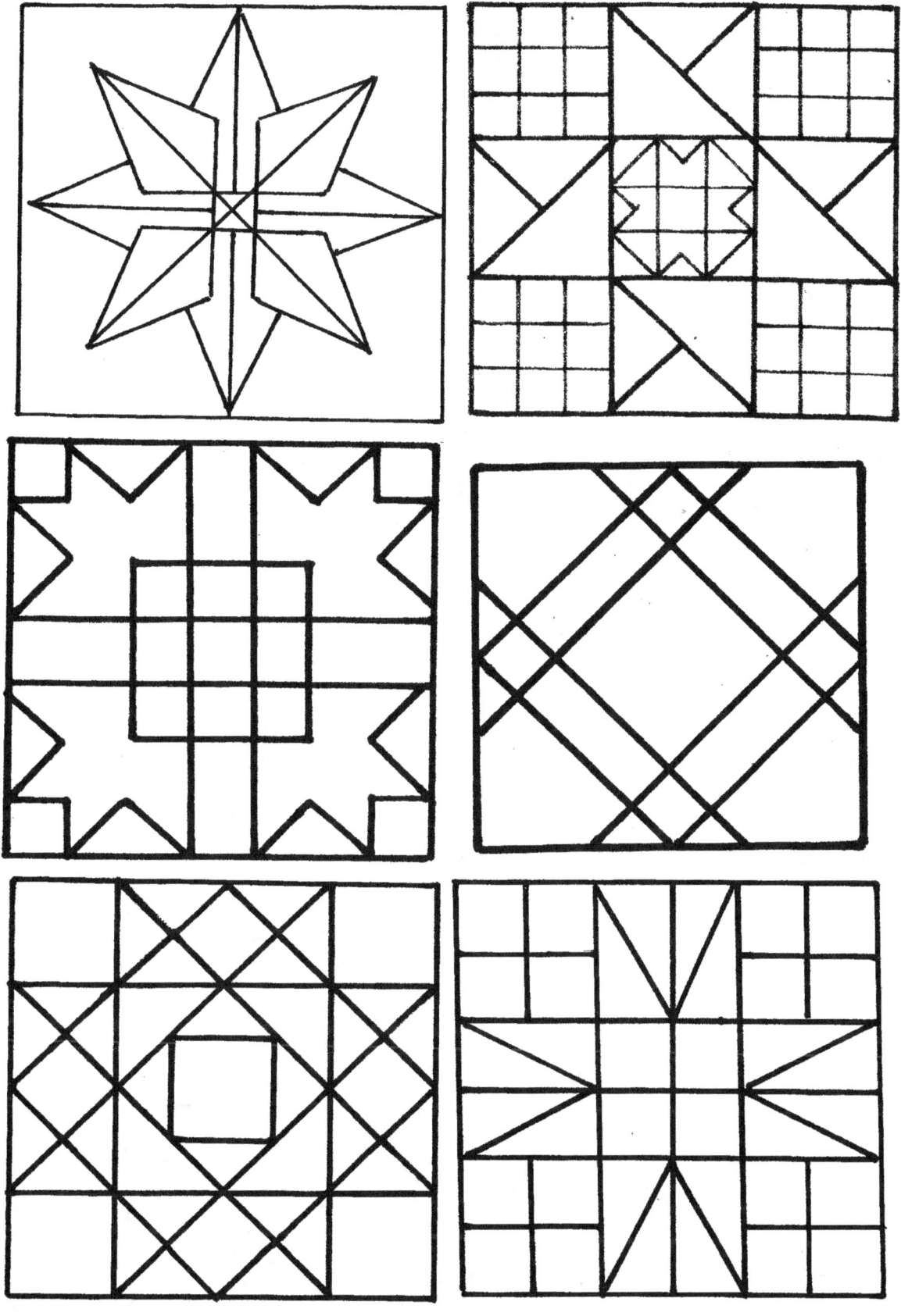

Barn Quilt Patterns

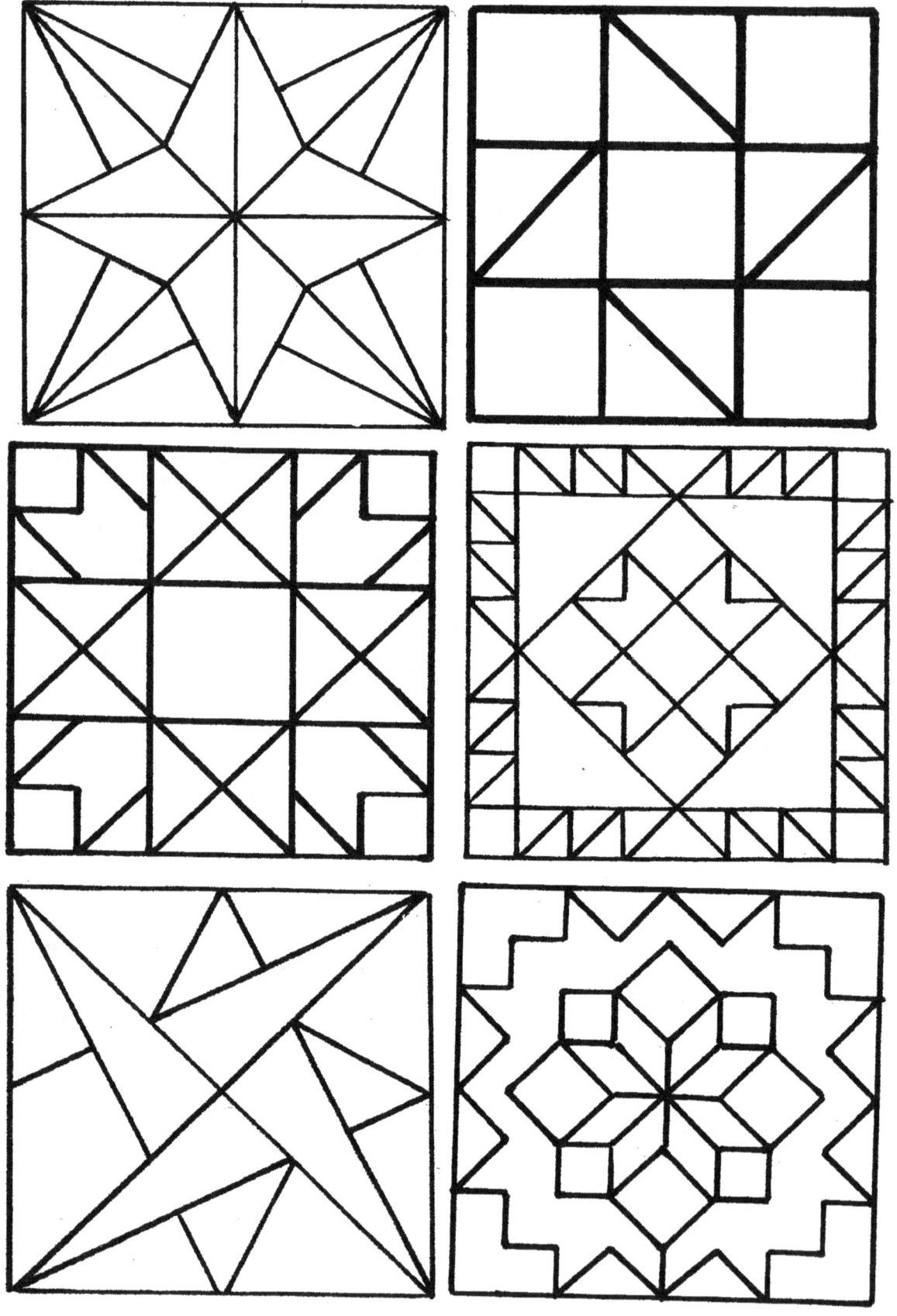

Barn Quilt Patterns

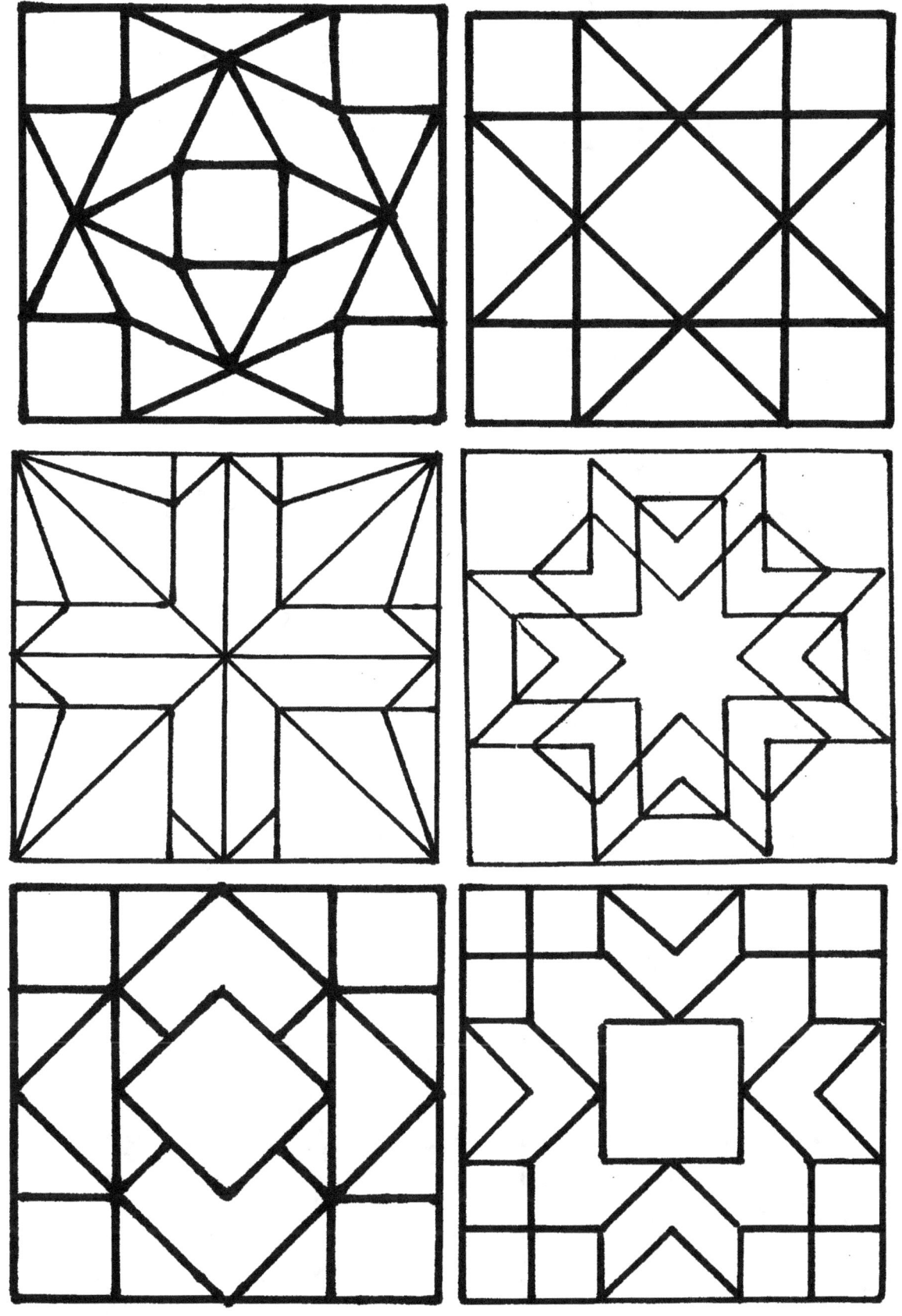

Barn Quilt Patterns

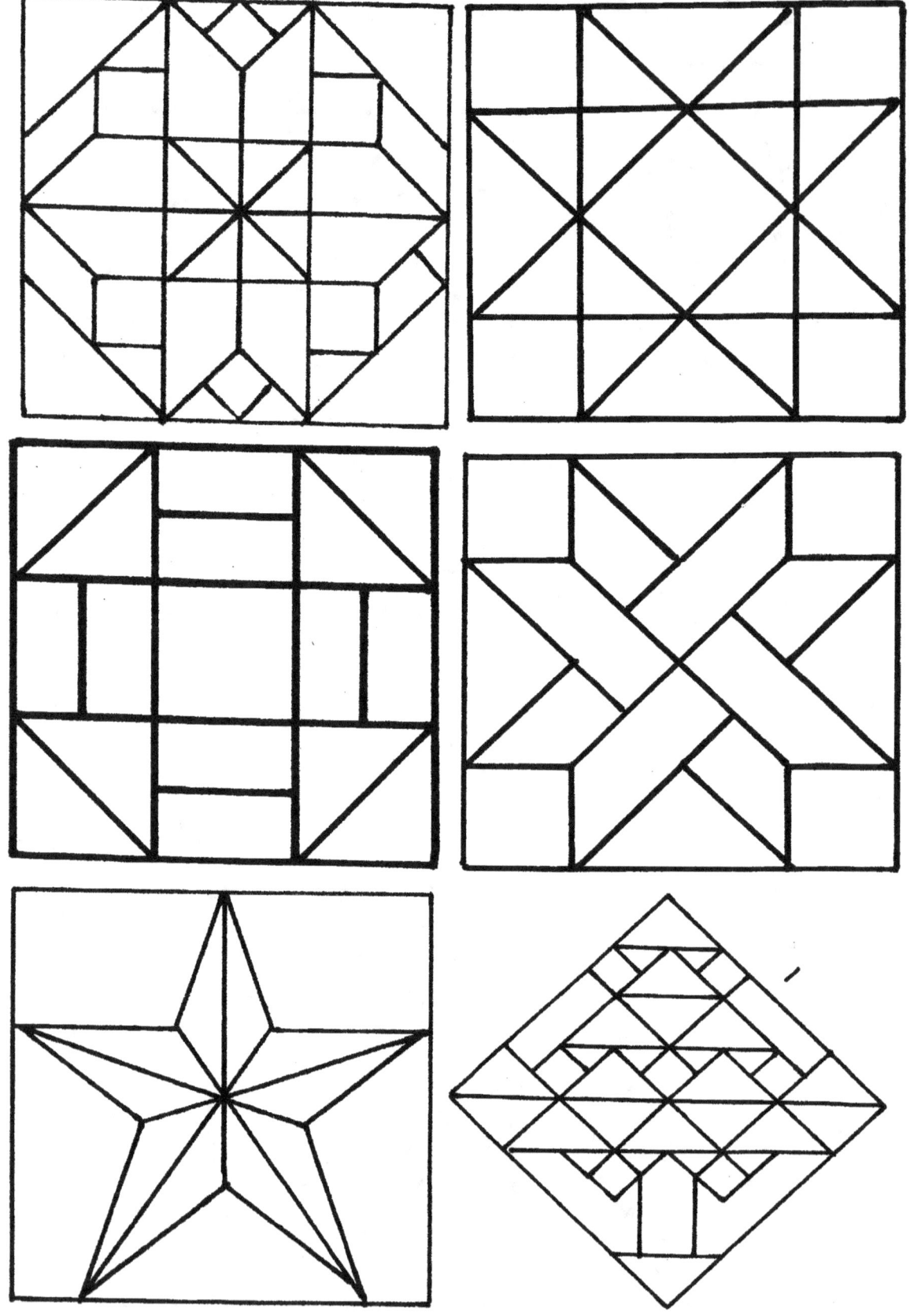

Barn Quilt Patterns

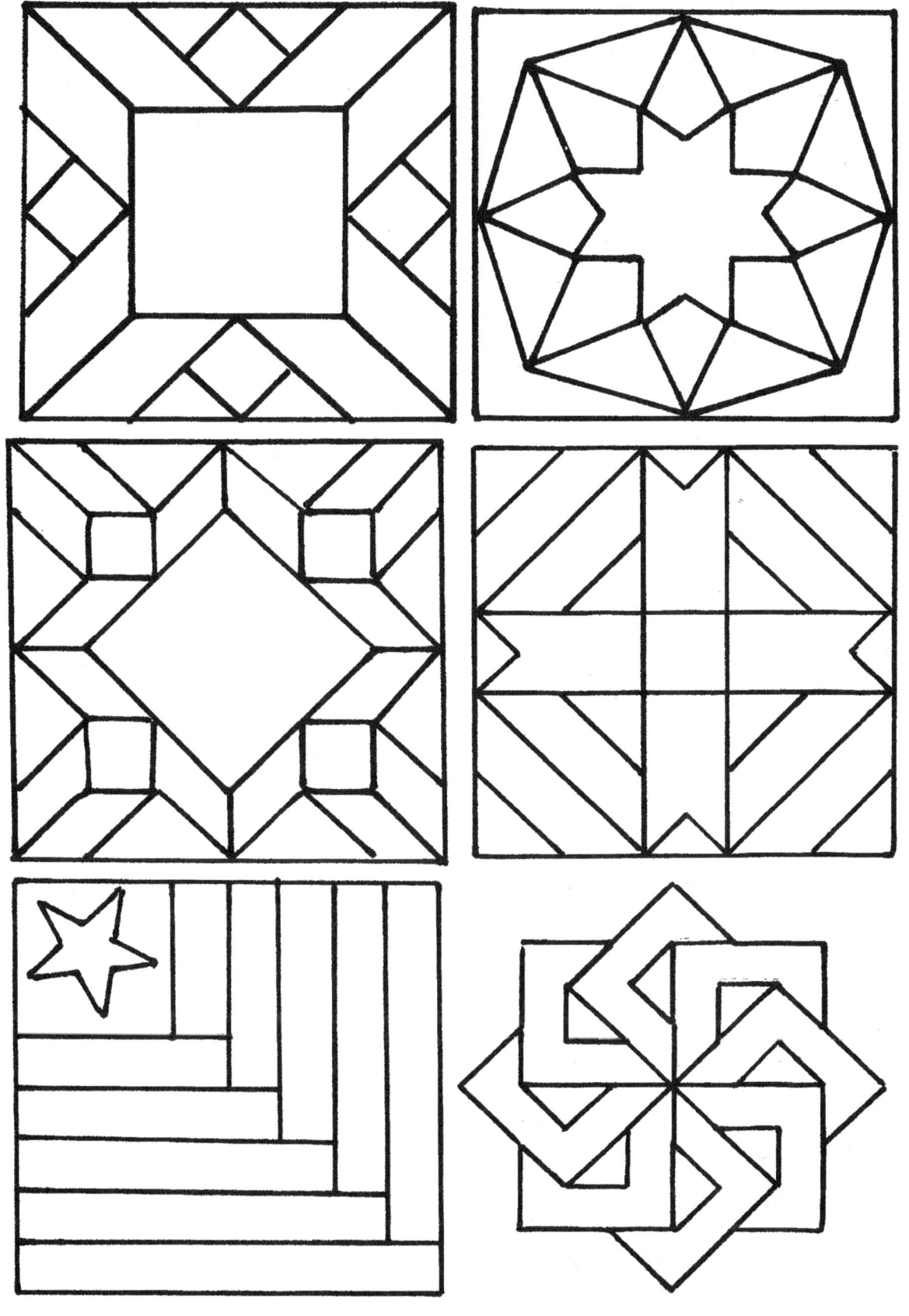

Barn Quilt Patterns

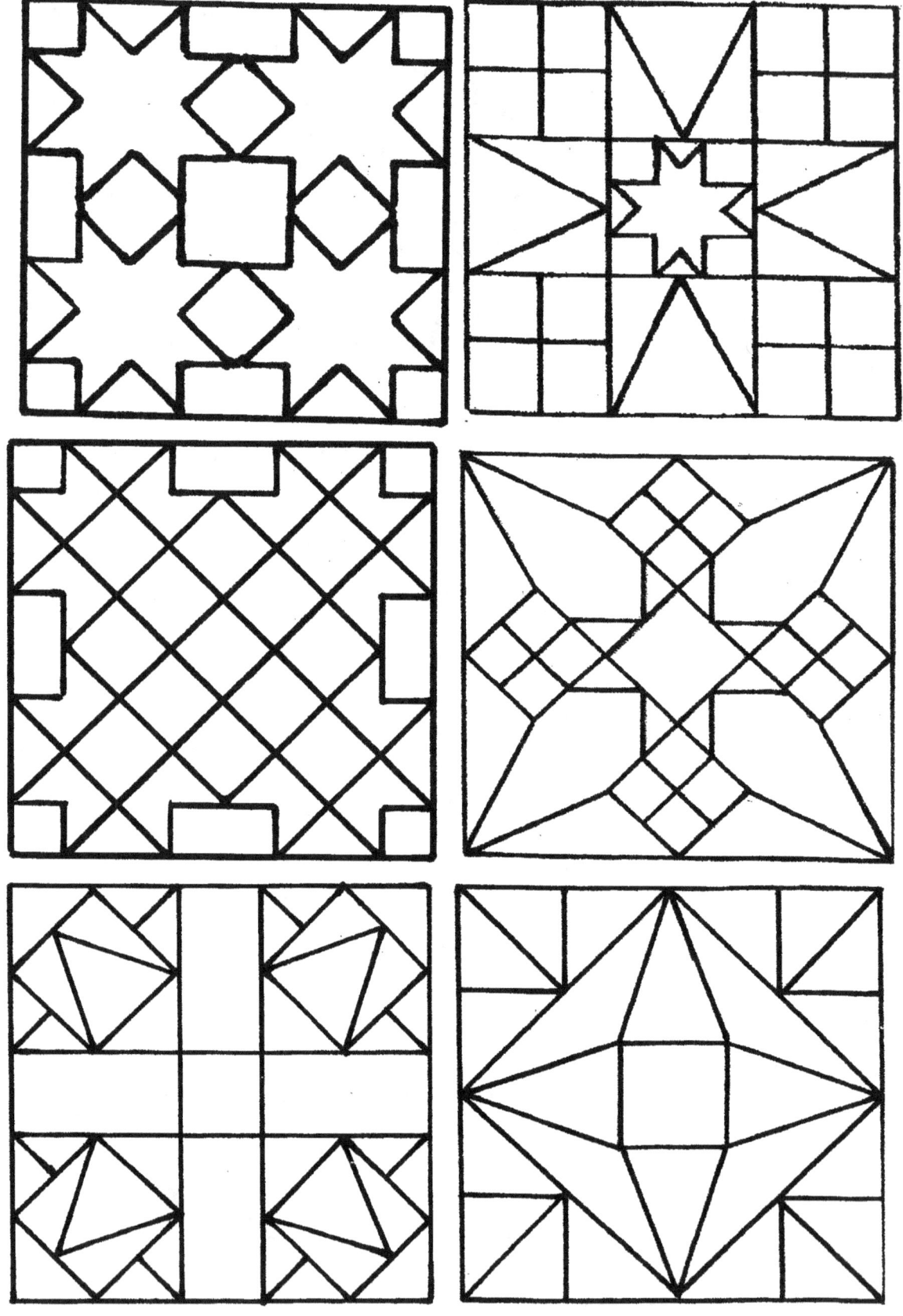

Barn Quilt Patterns

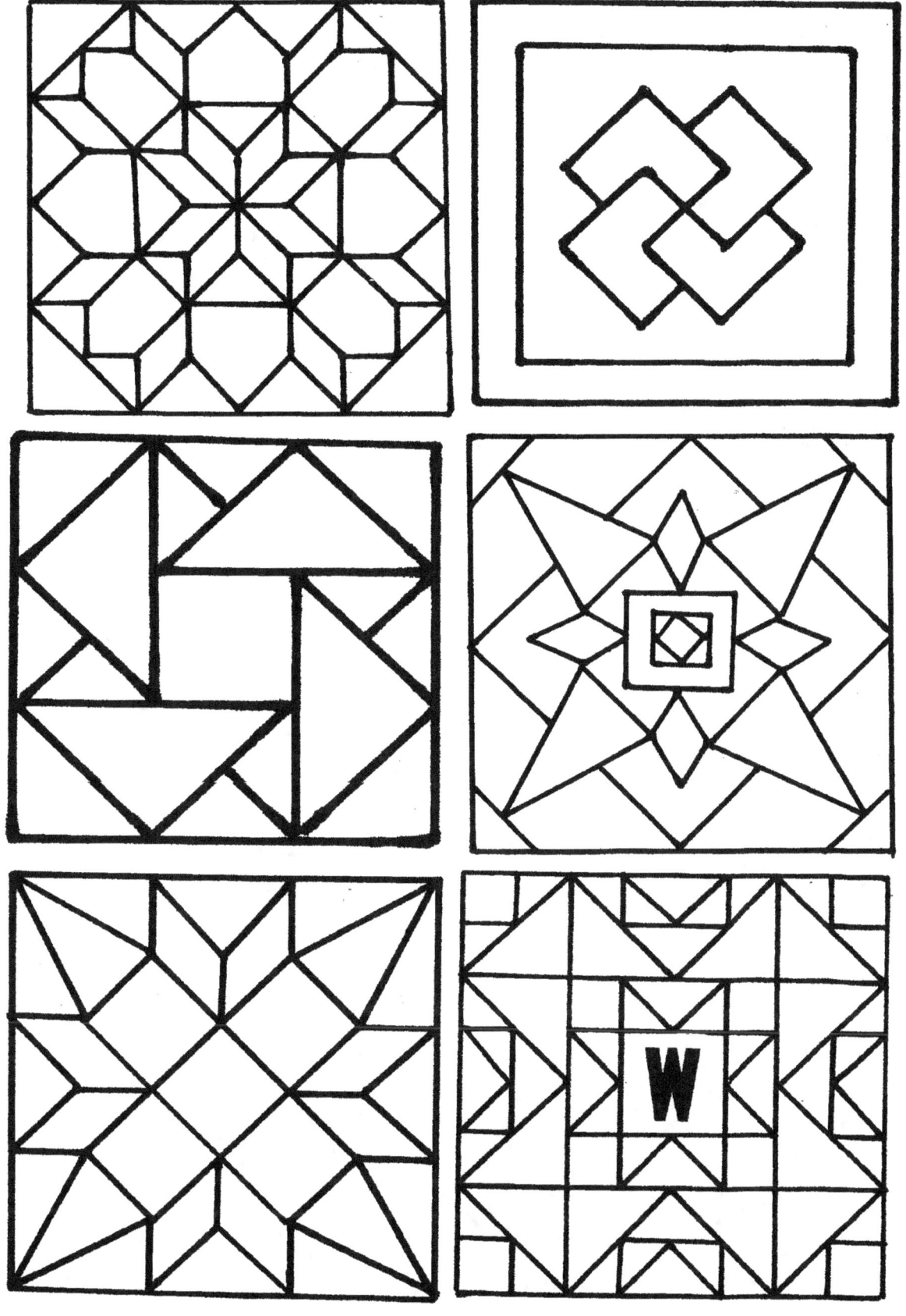

Barn Quilt Patterns

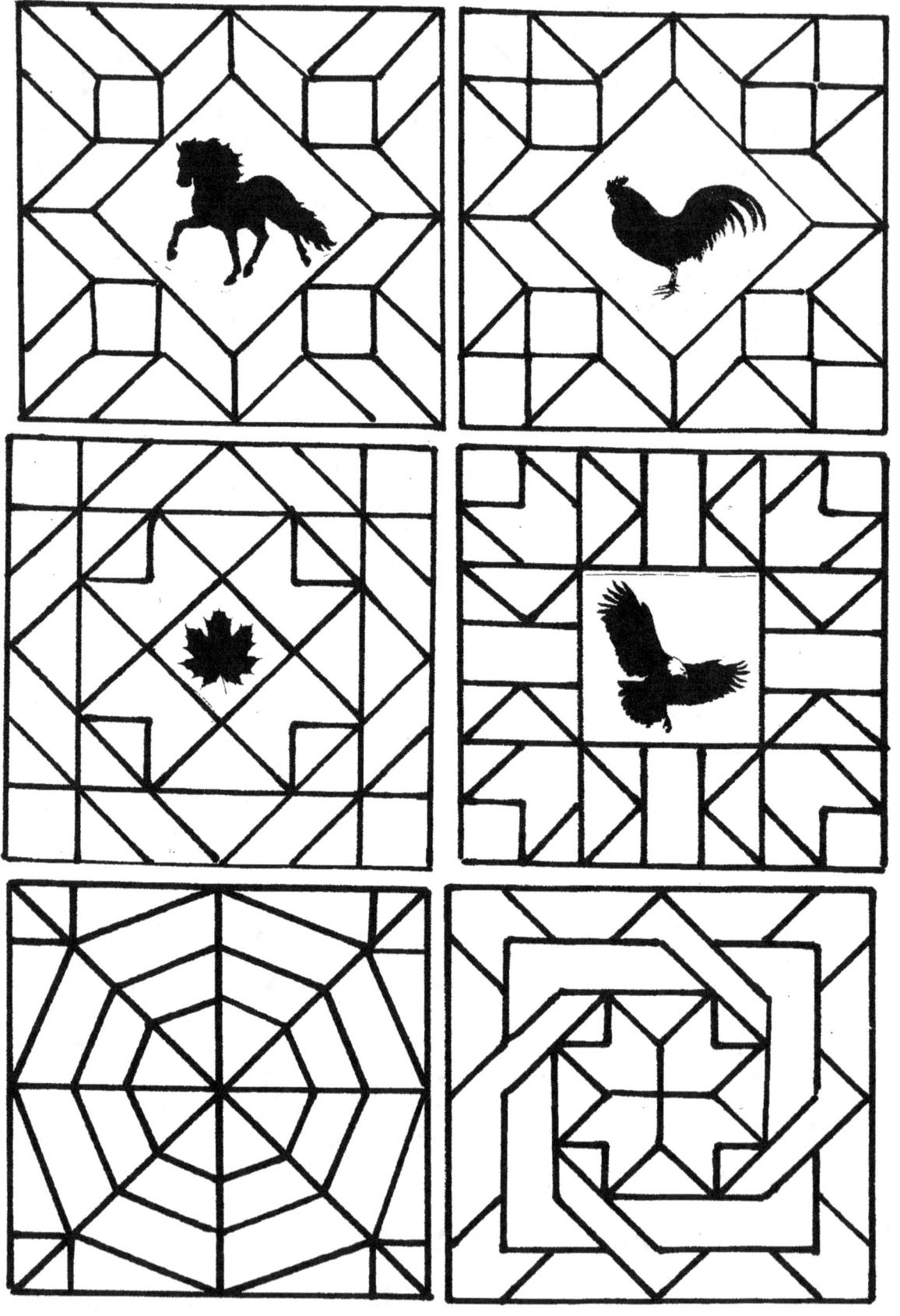

Barn Quilt Patterns

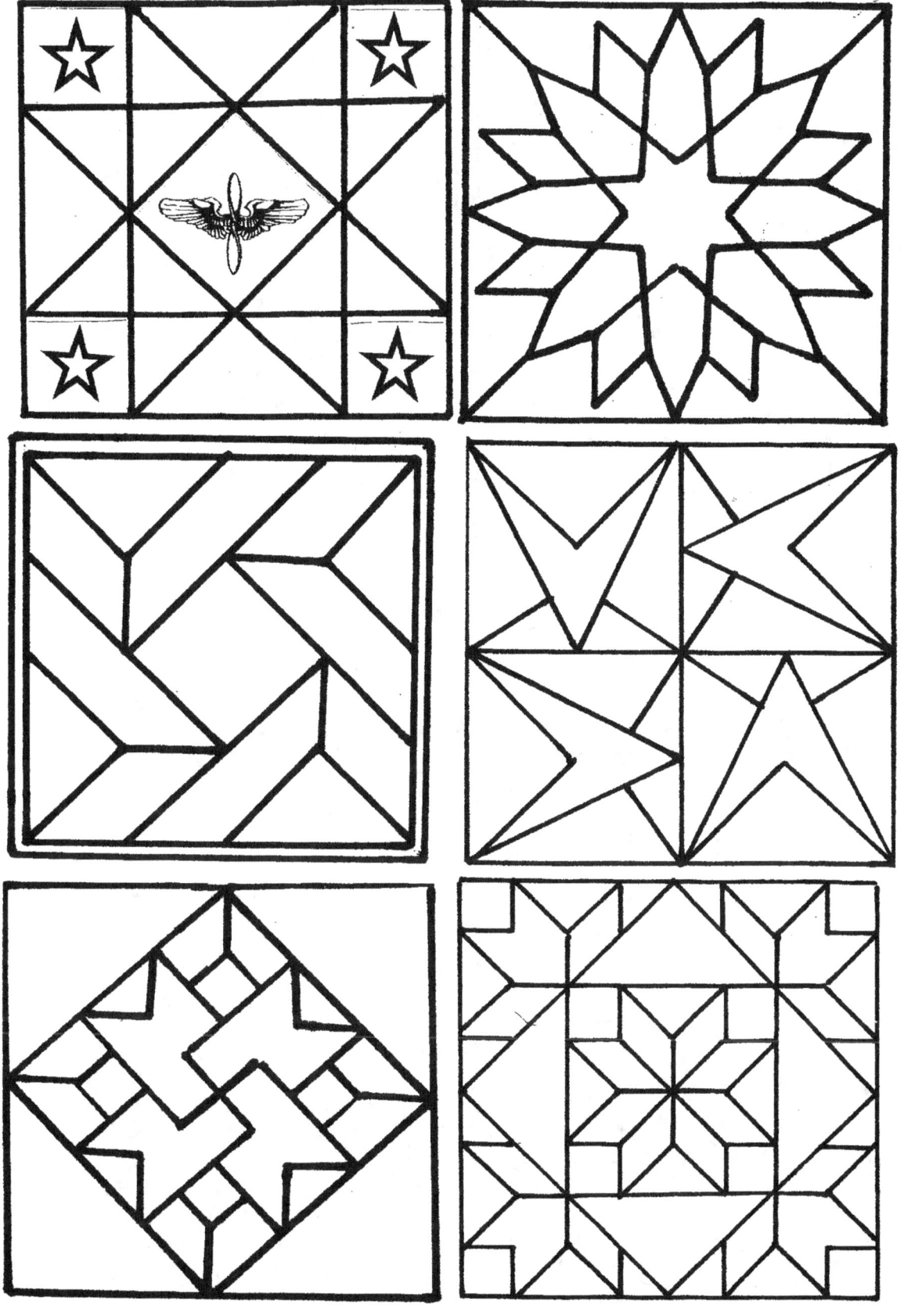

Barn Quilt Patterns

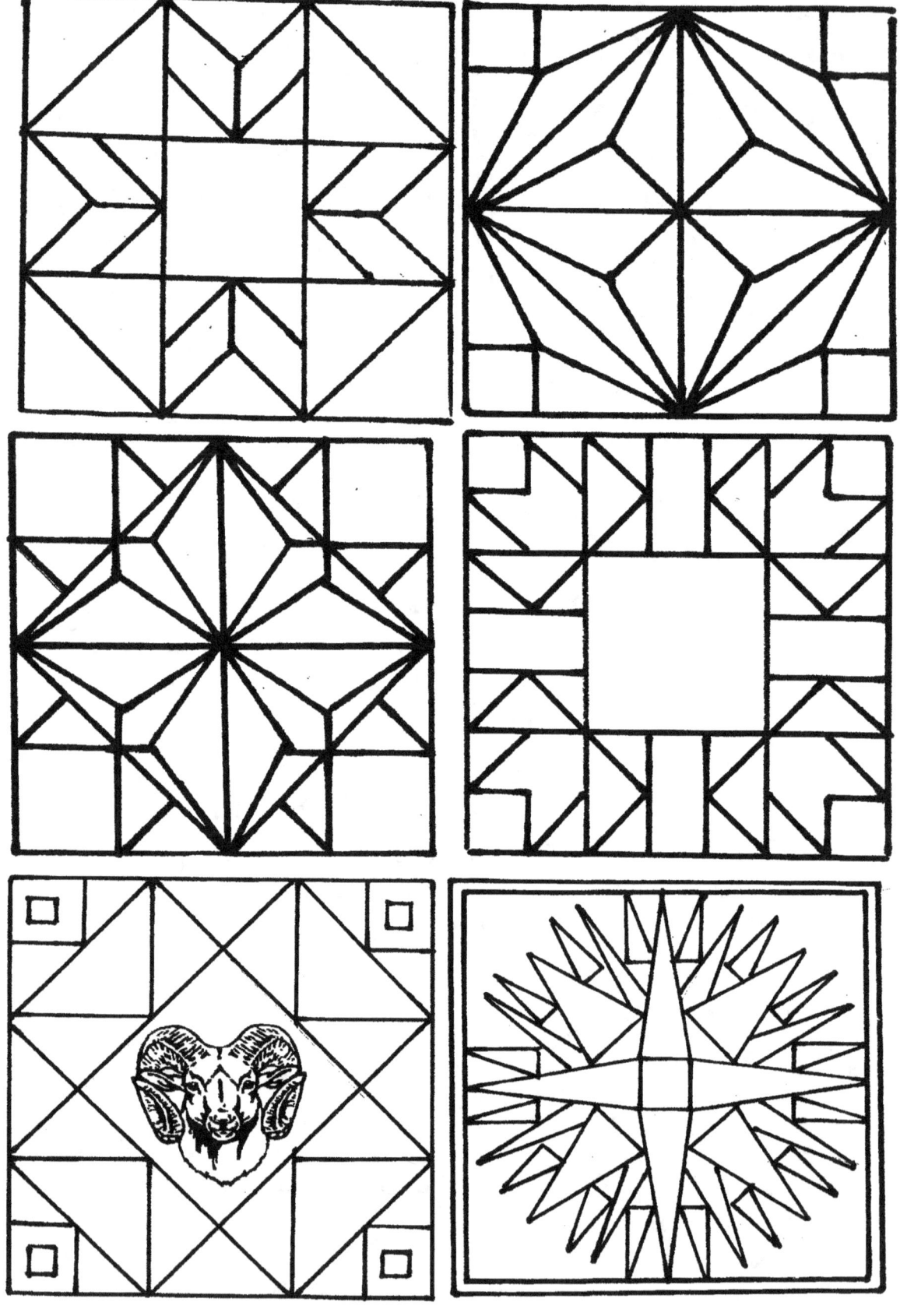

Barn Quilt Patterns

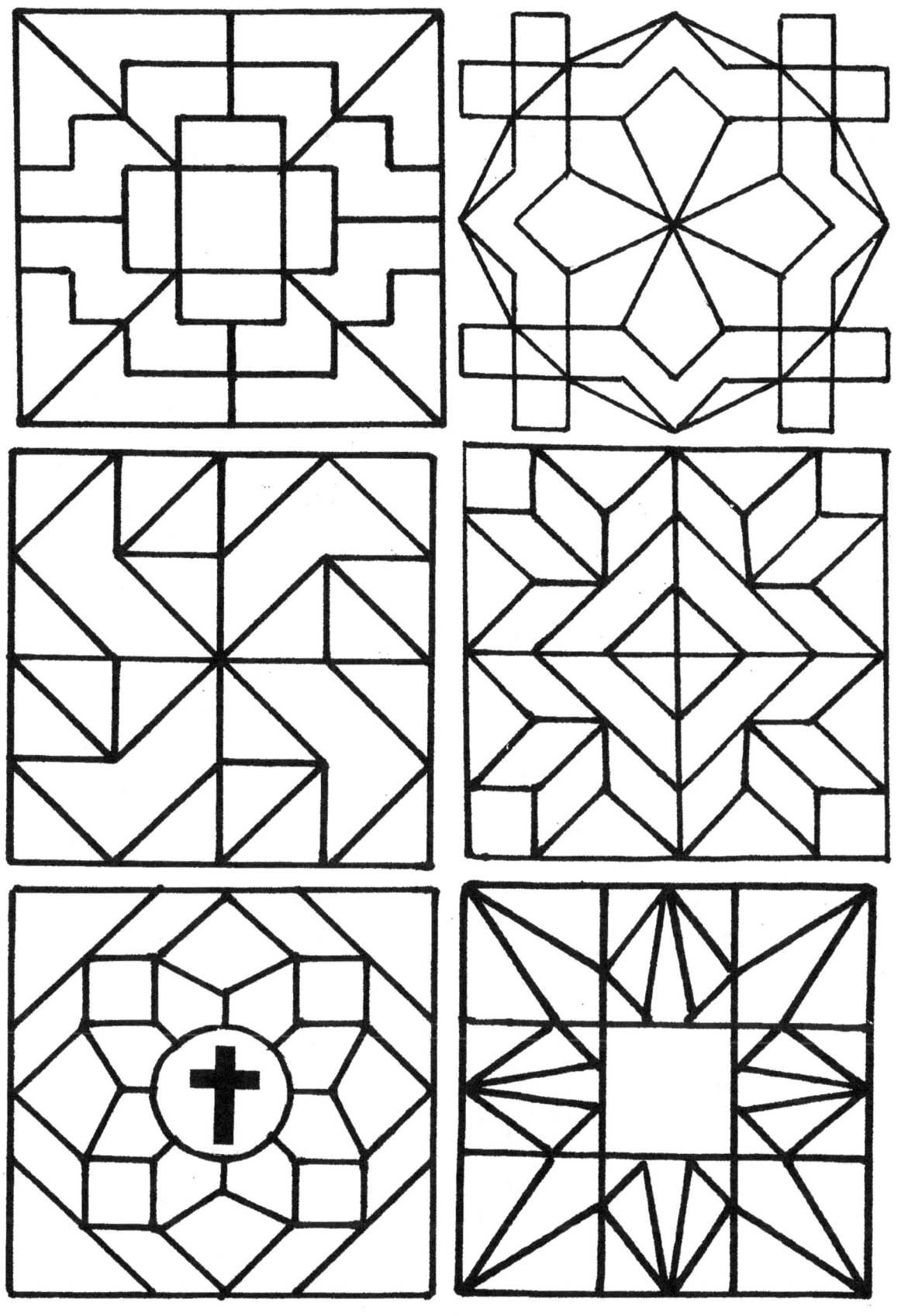

Barn Quilt Patterns

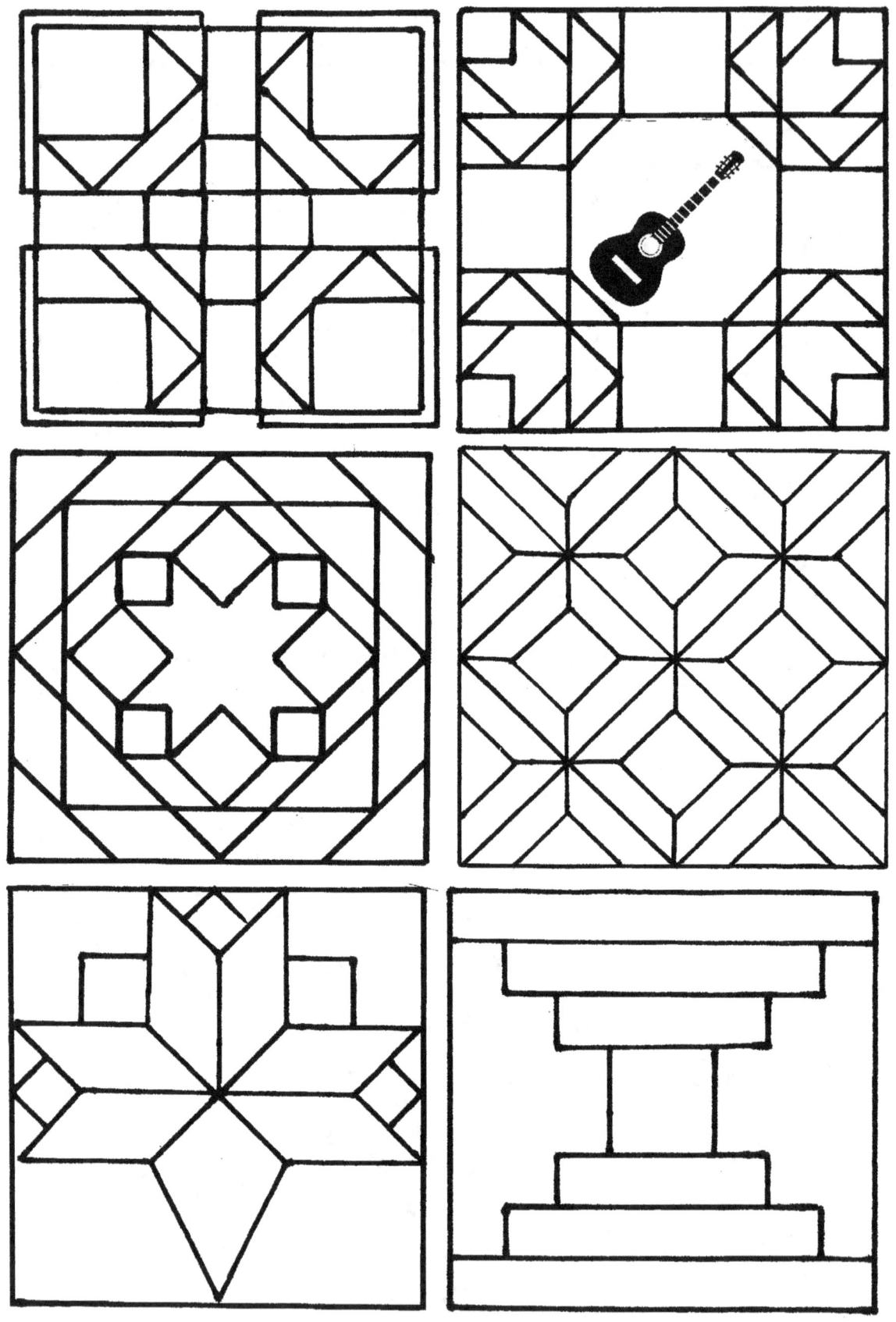

Barn Quilt Patterns

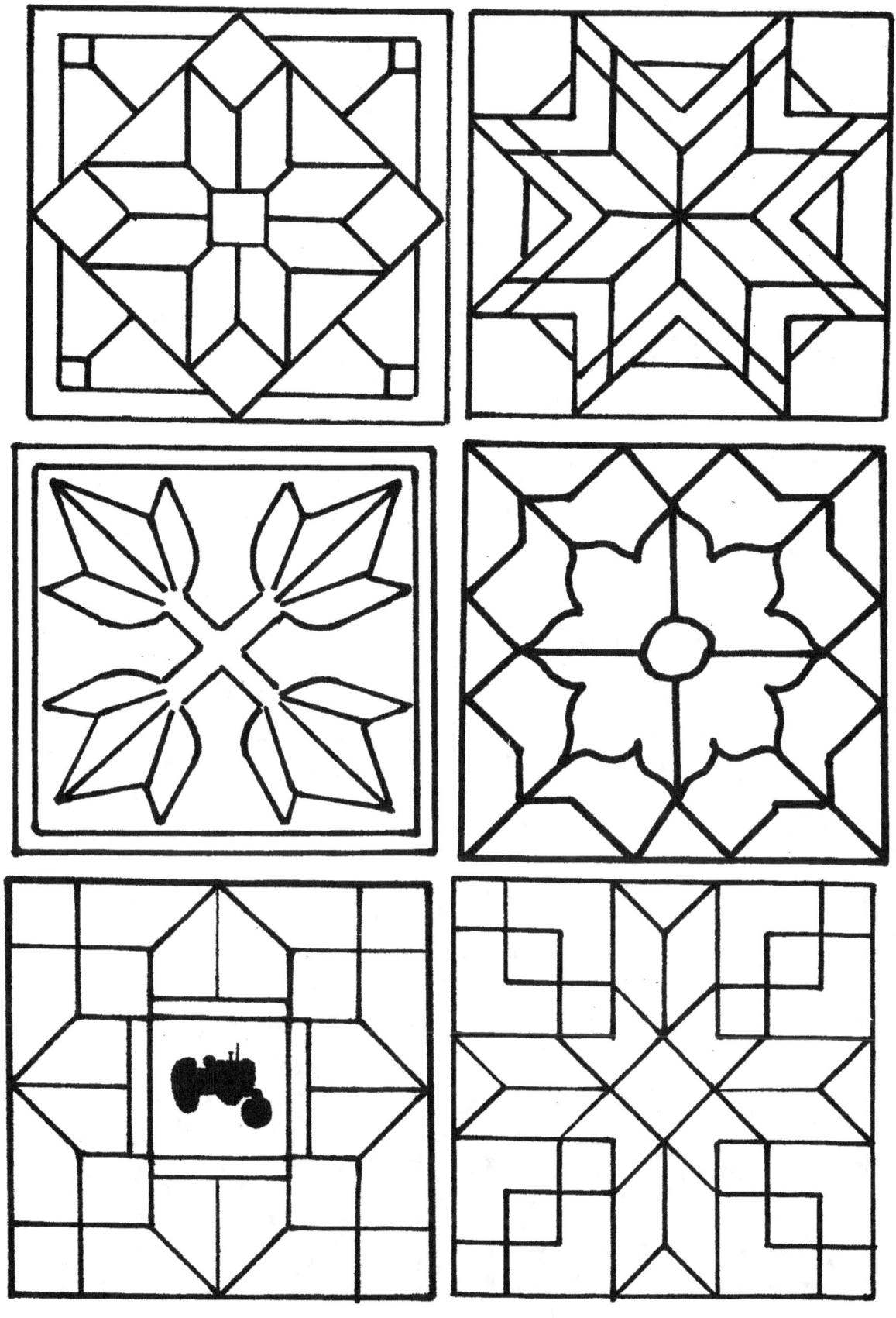

Barn Quilt Patterns

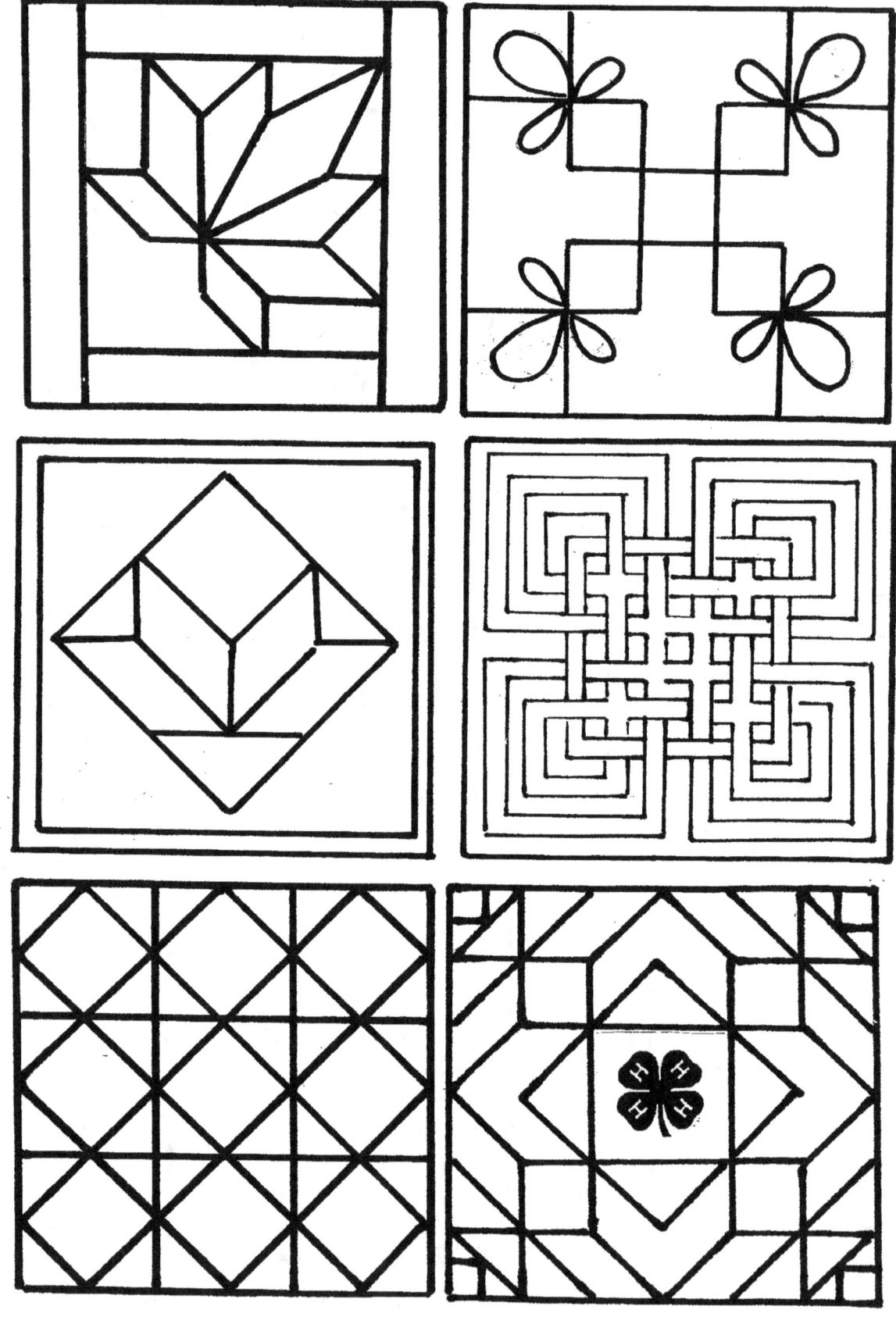

Barn Quilt Patterns

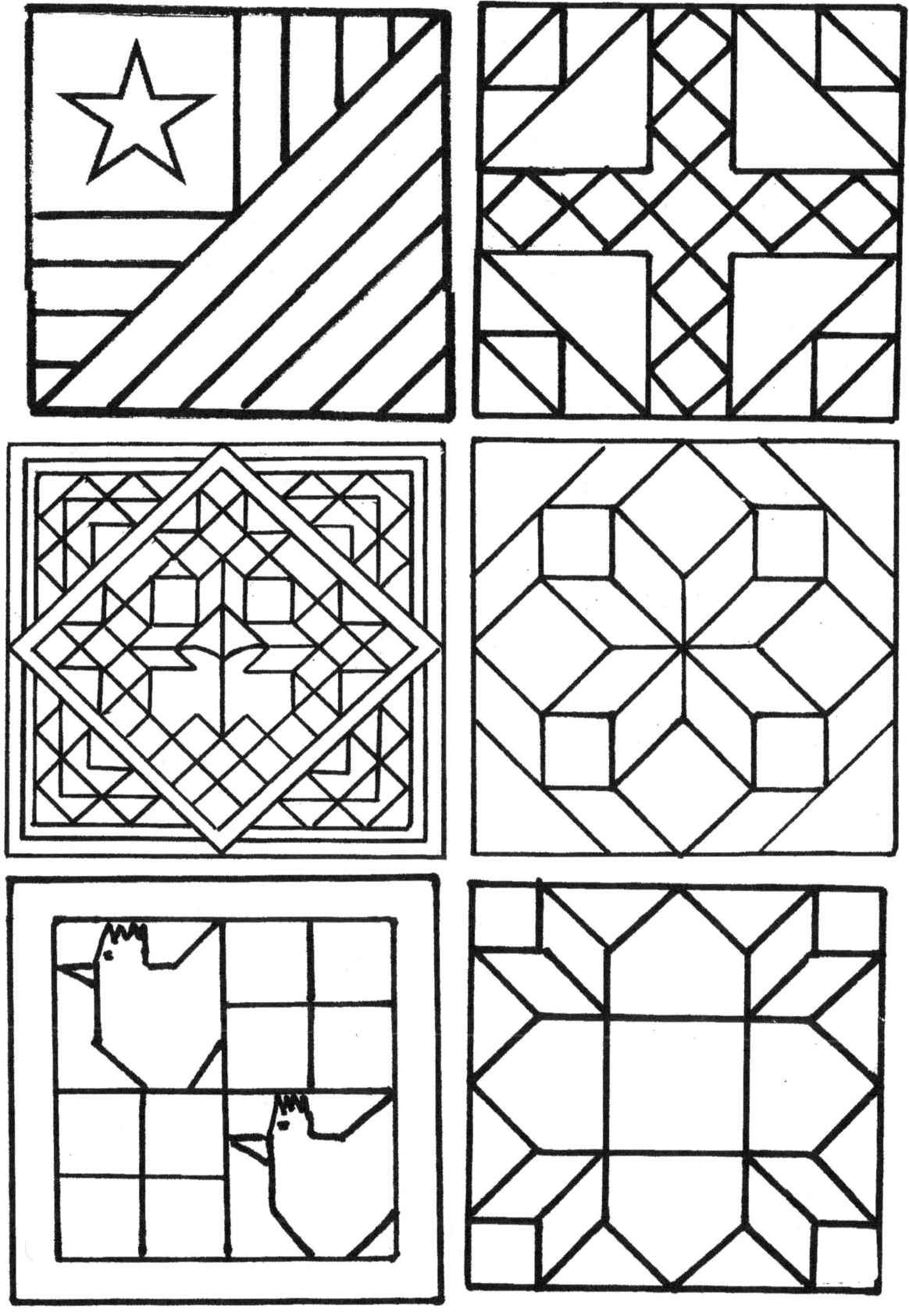

Barn Quilt Patterns

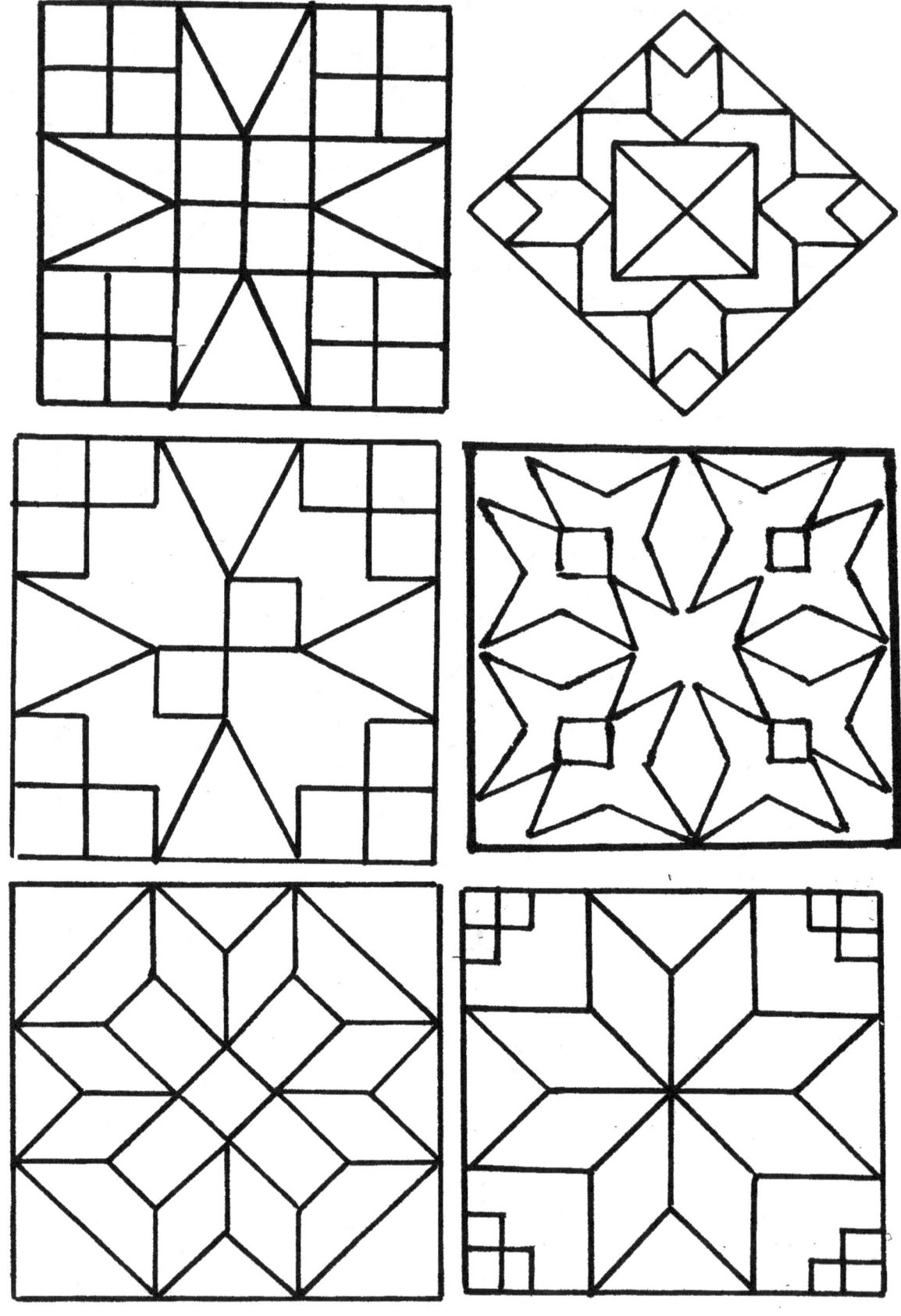

Barn Quilt Patterns

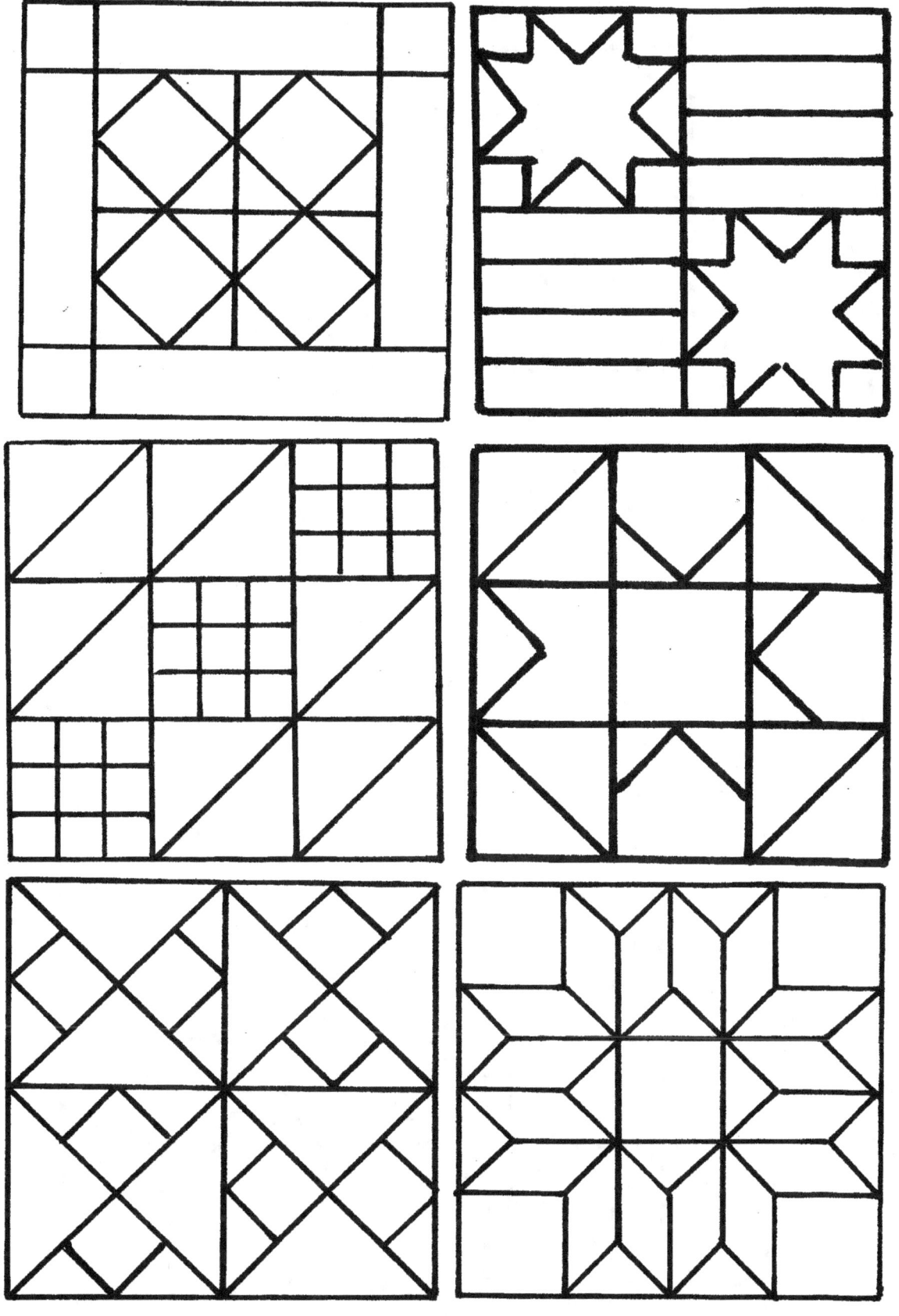

Barn Quilt Patterns

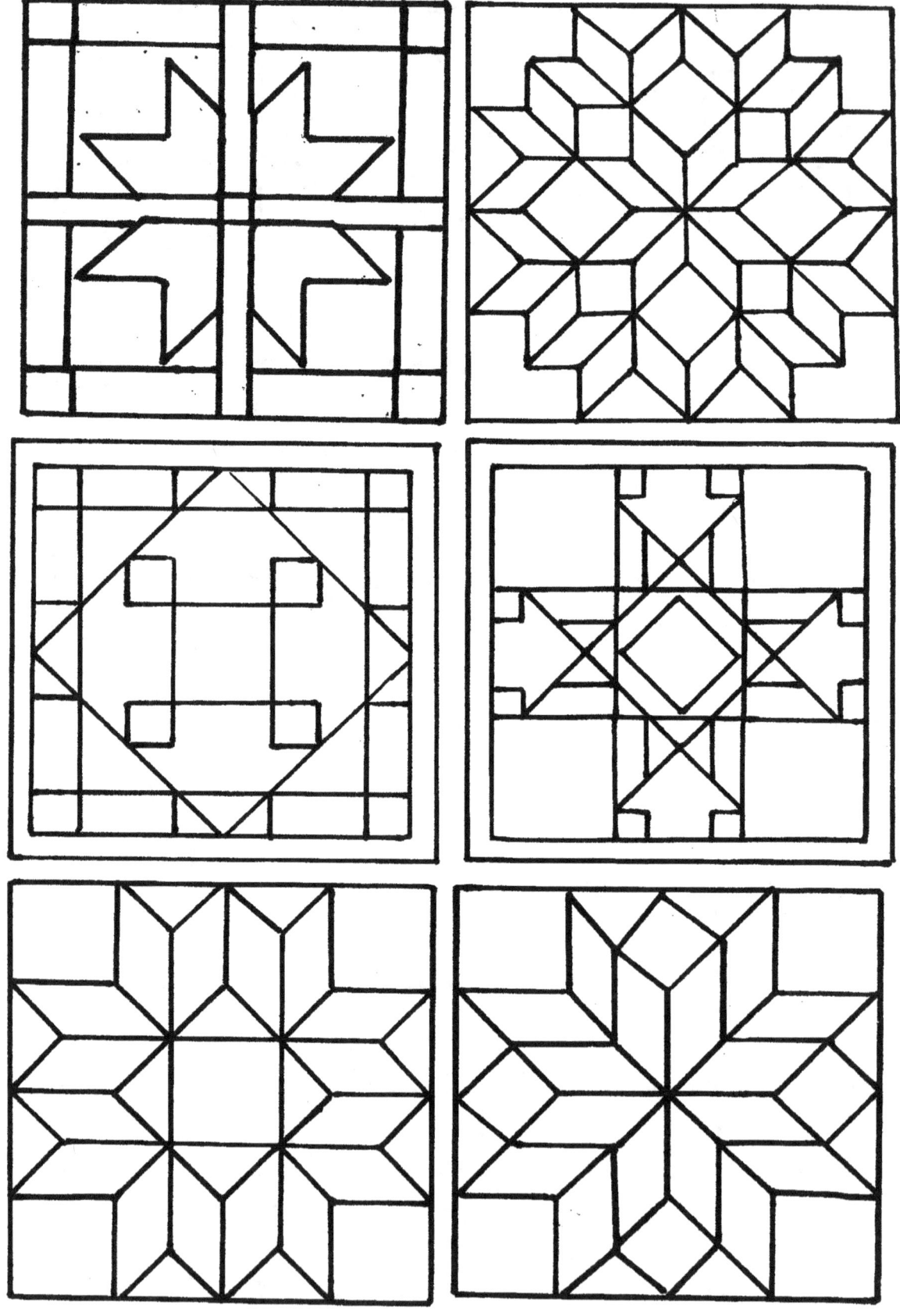

Barn Quilt Patterns

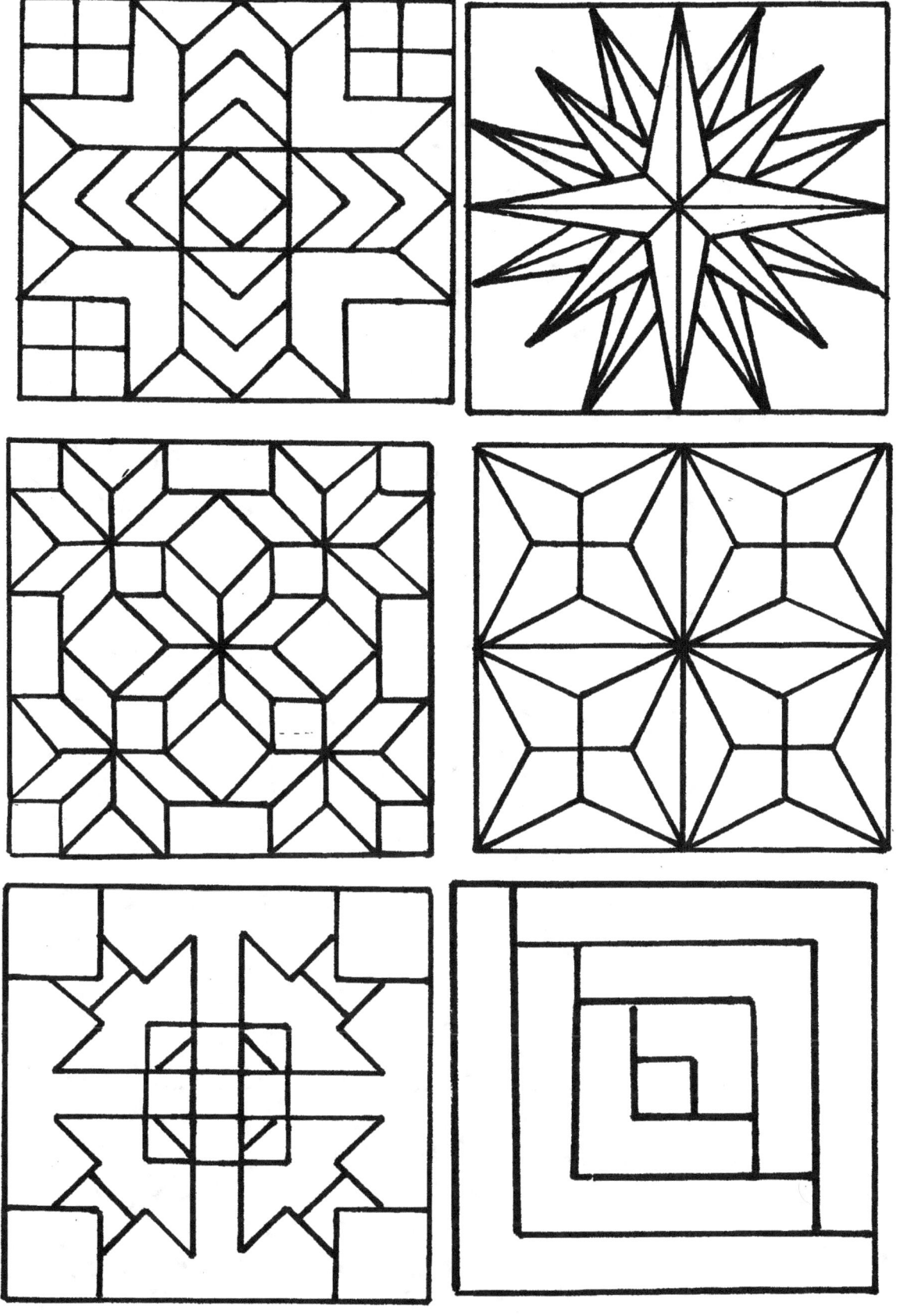

Barn Quilt Patterns

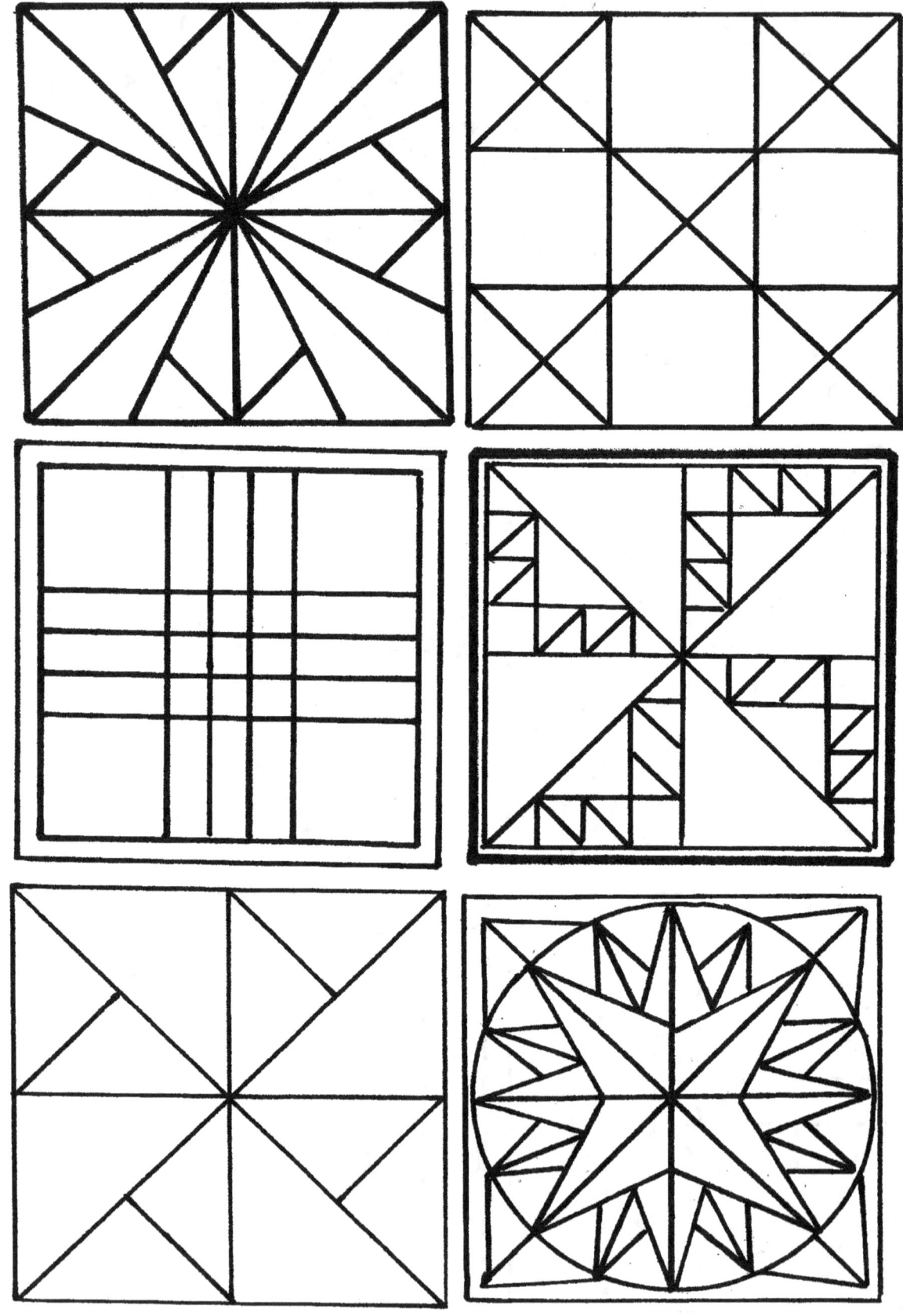

Barn Quilt Patterns

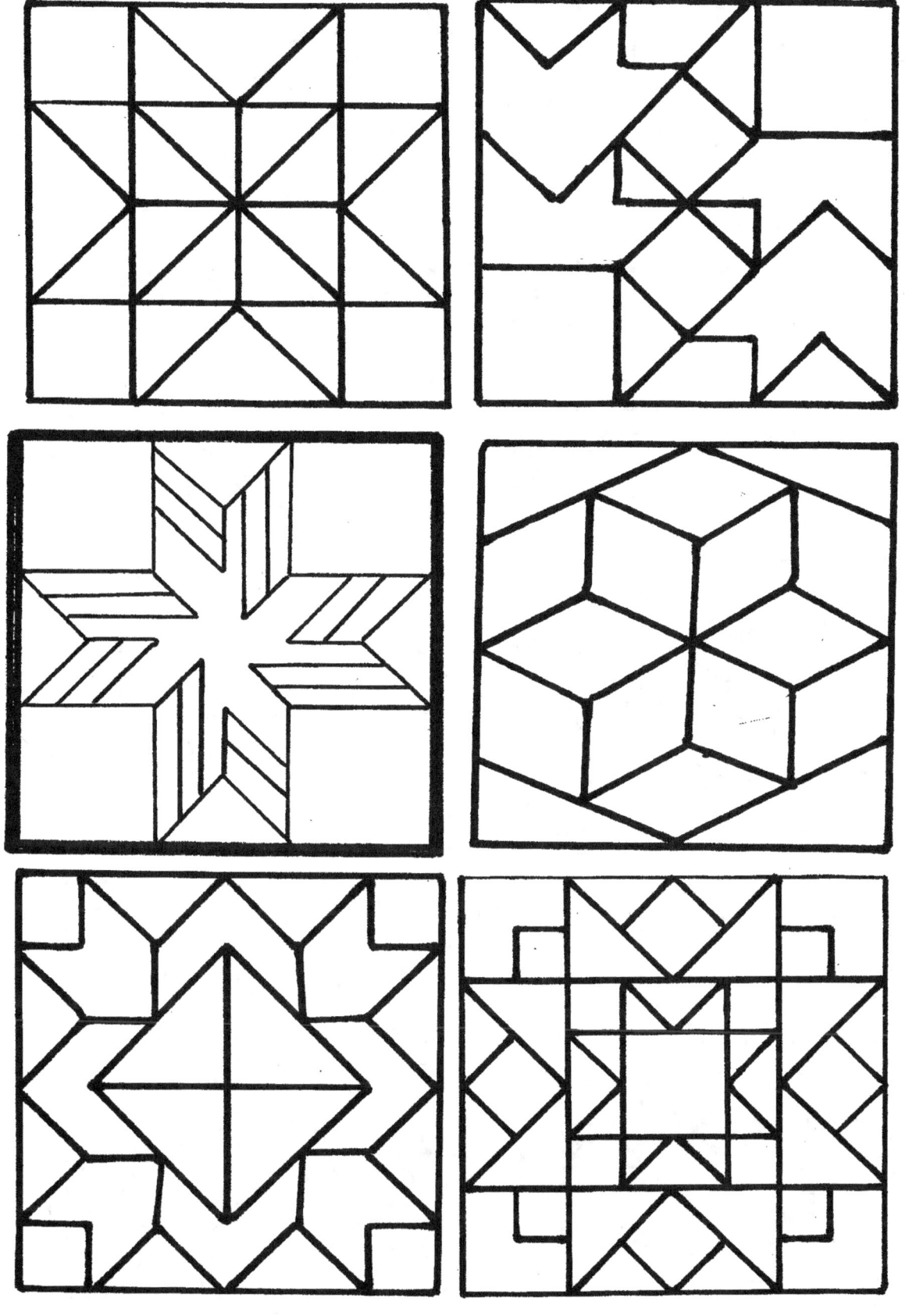

Barn Quilt Patterns

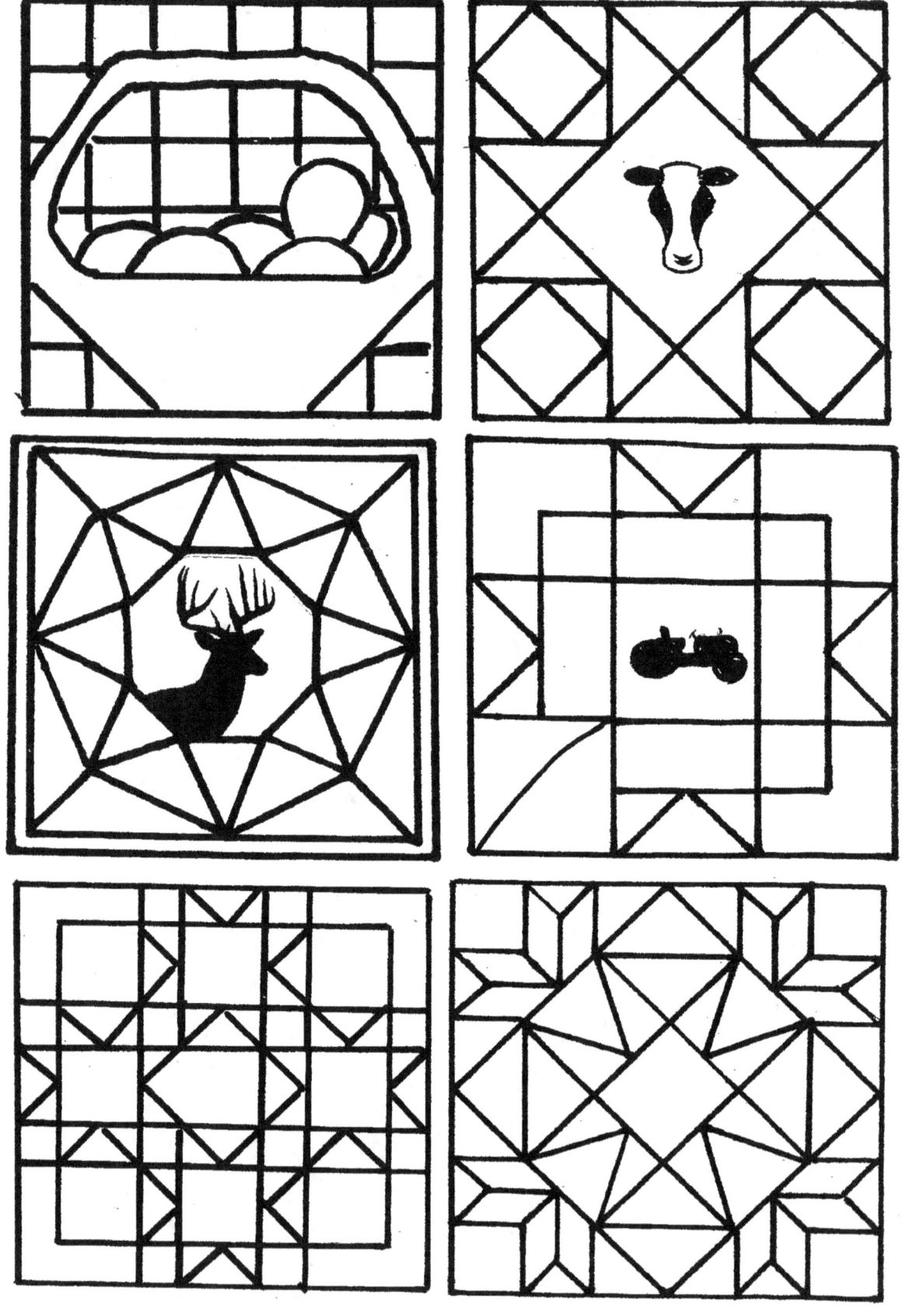

Barn Quilt Patterns

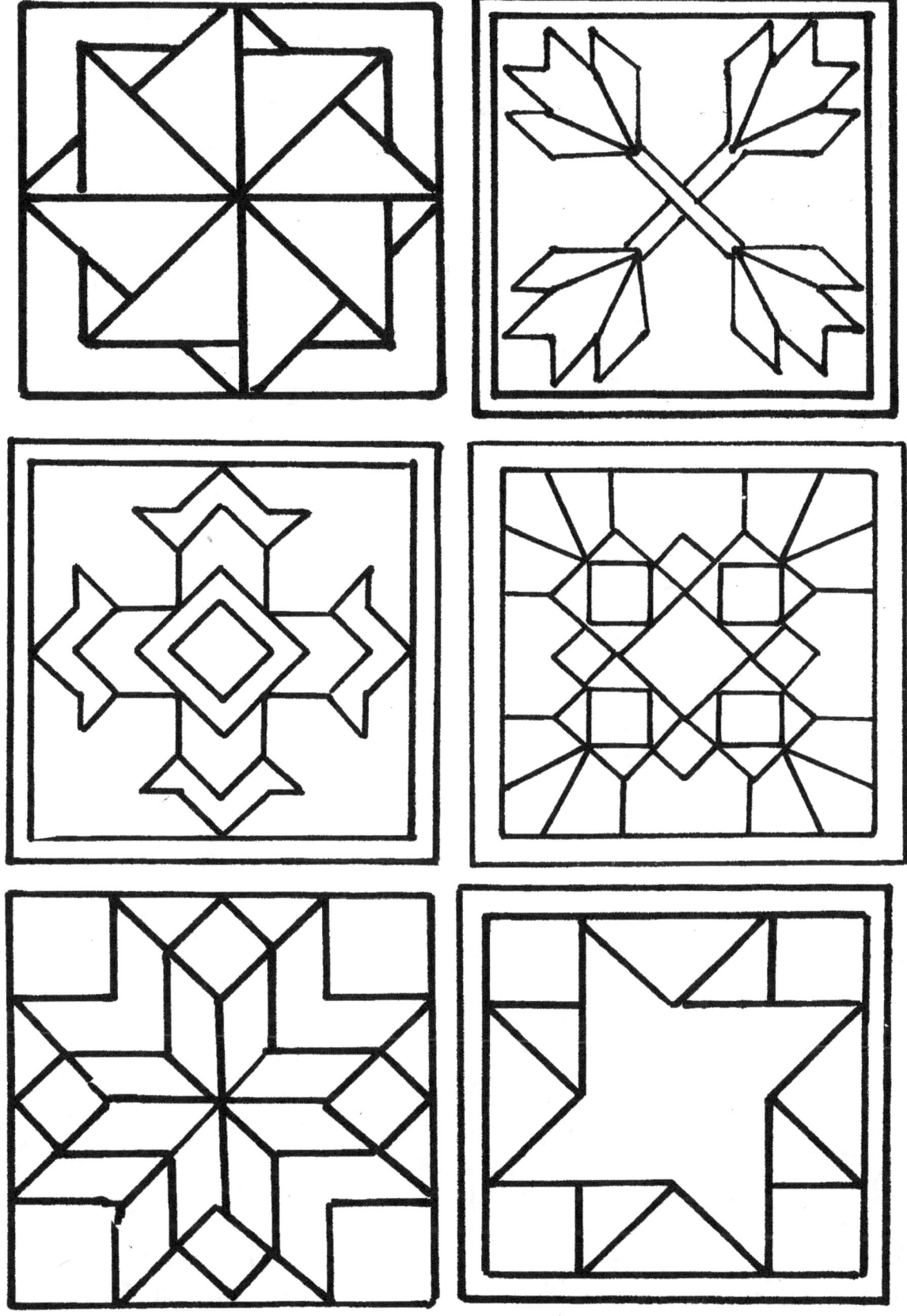

Barn Quilt Patterns

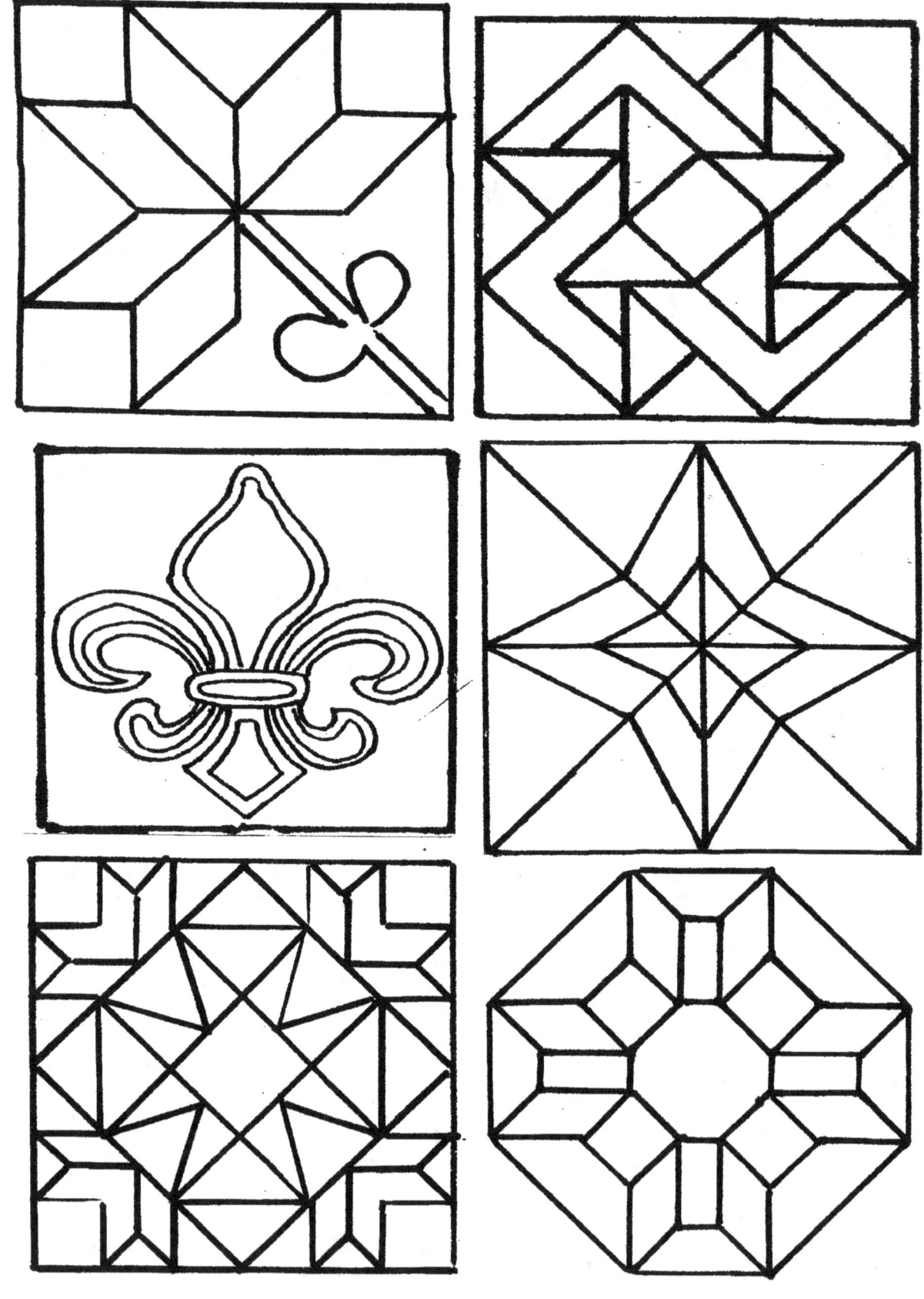

Barn Quilt Patterns

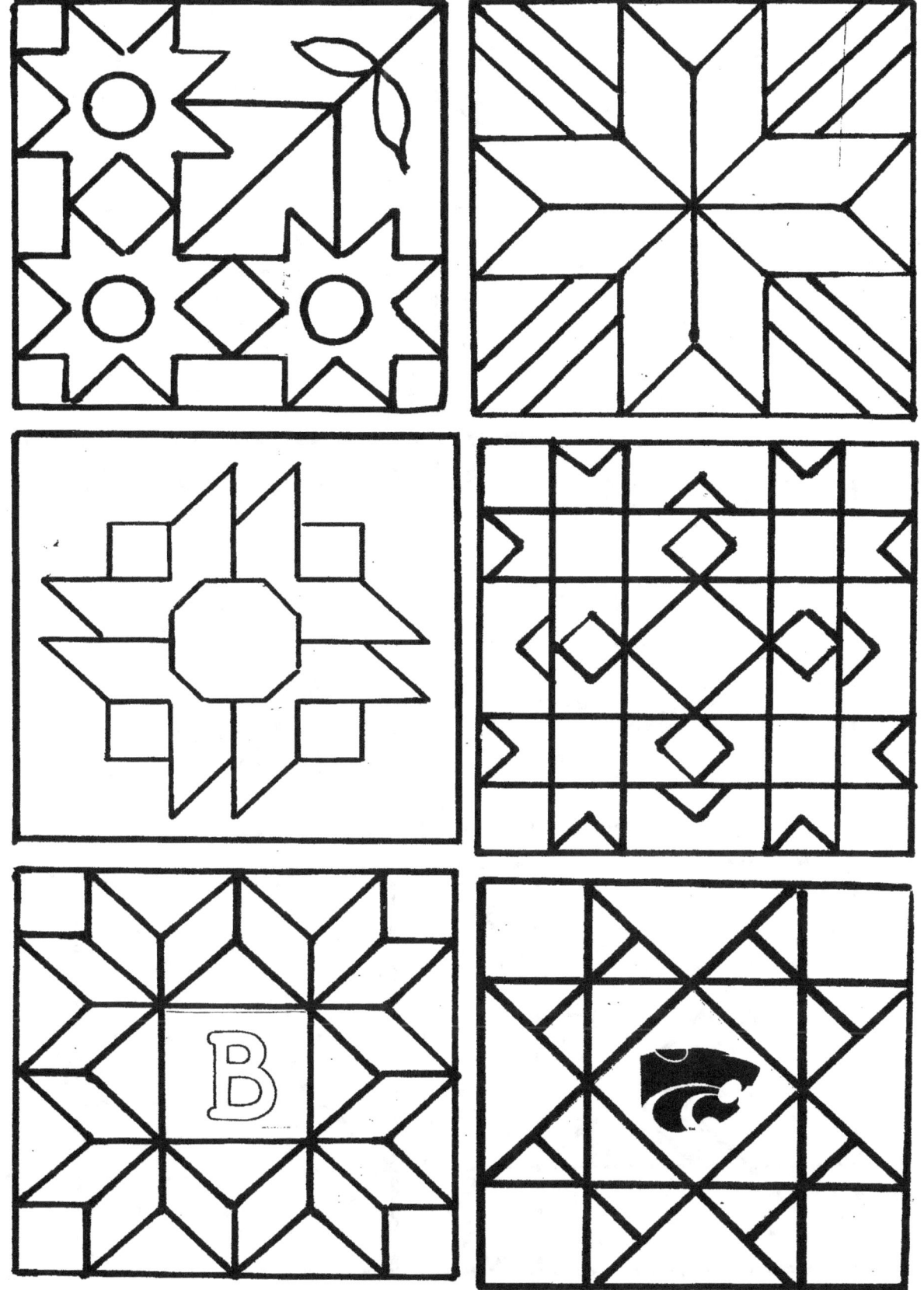

Barn Quilt Patterns

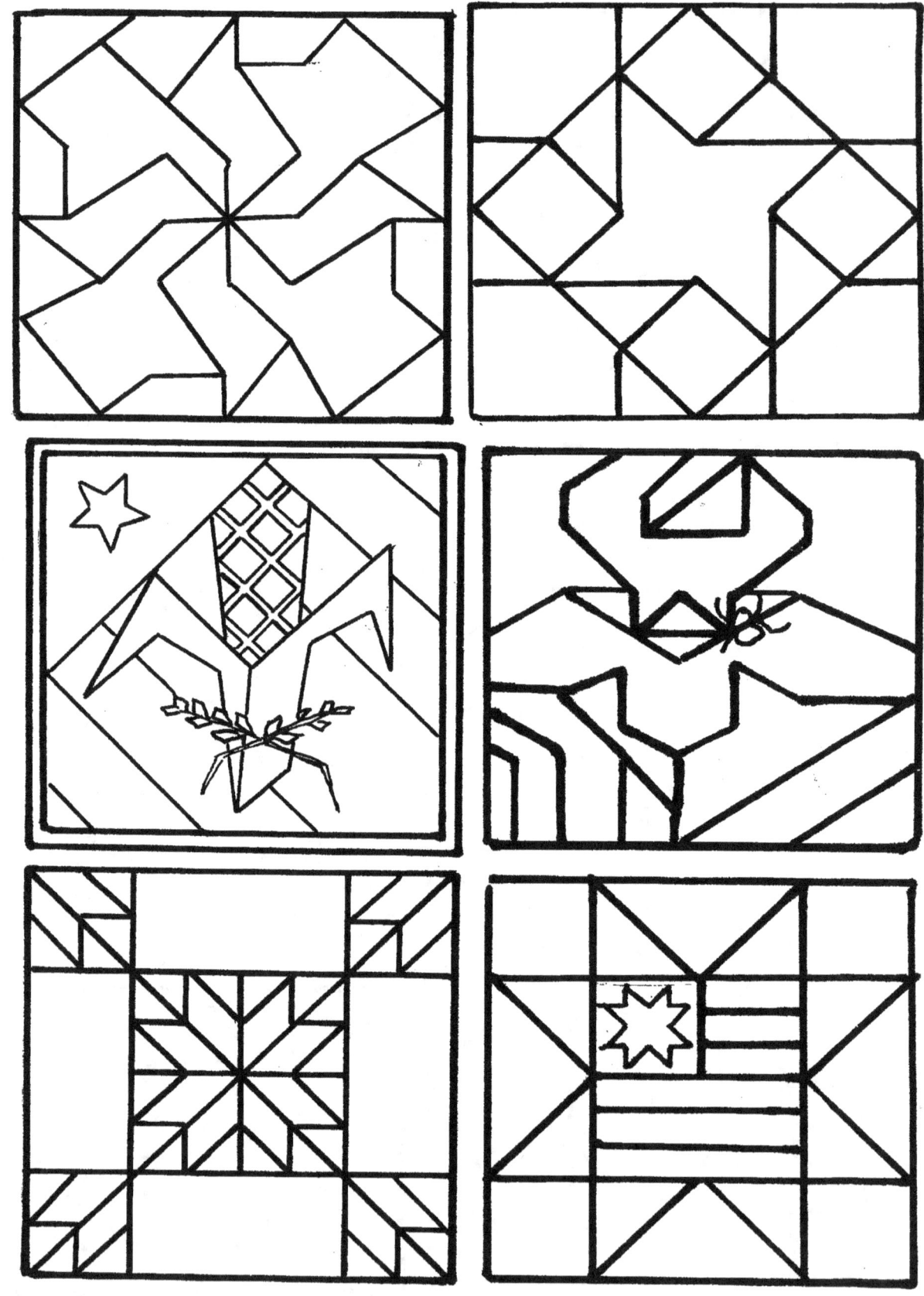

Barn Quilt Patterns

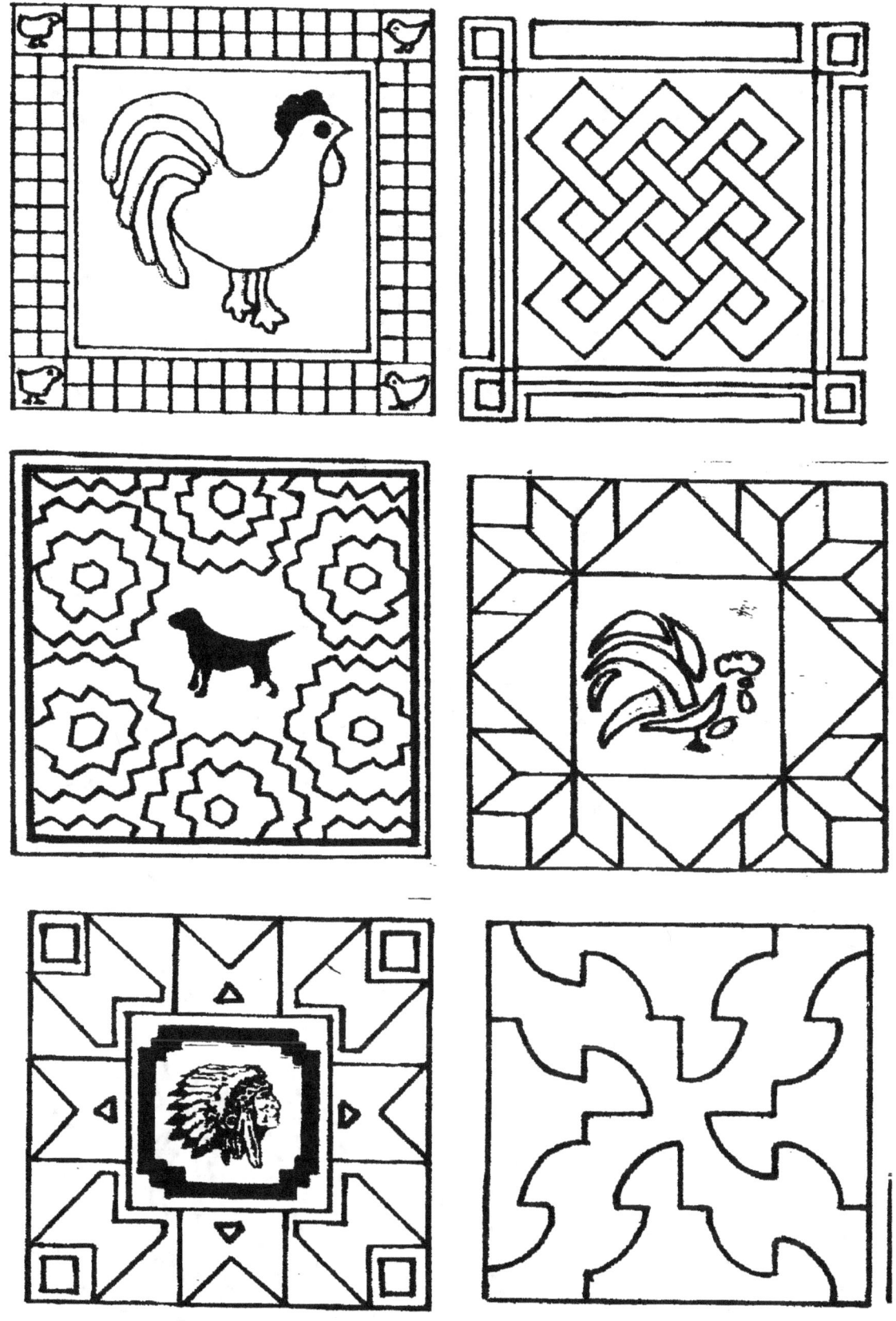

Barn Quilt Patterns

Barn Quilt Patterns

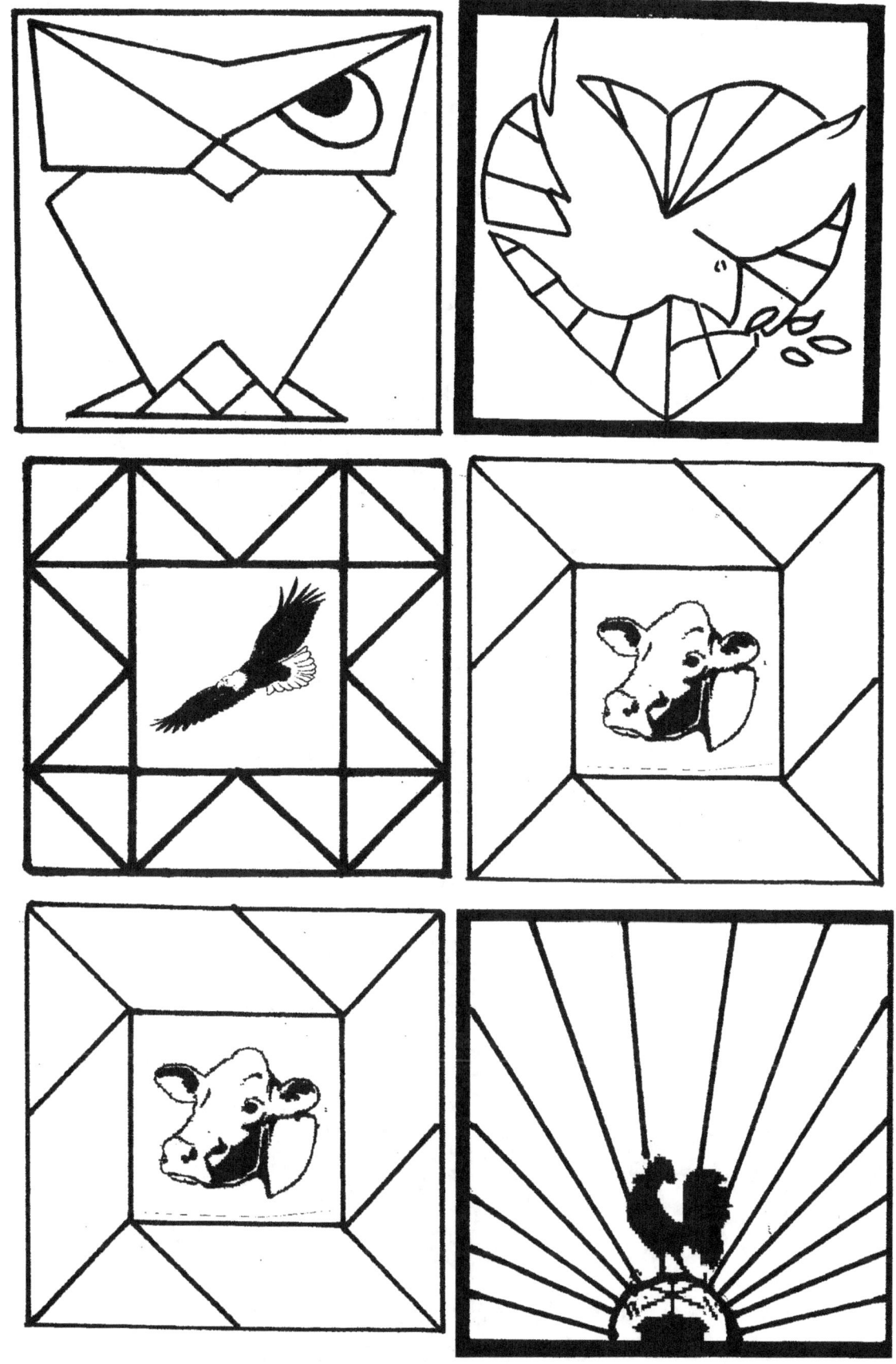

John Lettau Coloring Books

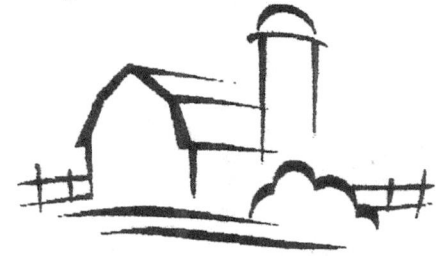

Barn Quilt Coloring Books

Shawano County Wisconsin Barn Quilt Coloring Book One
Shawano County Wisconsin Barn Quilt Coloring Book Two
Green County Wisconsin Barn Quilt Coloring Book
Delaware County Iowa Barn Quilt Coloring Book
Tennessee Appalachian Barn Quilt Trail Coloring Book One
Tennessee Appalachian Barn Quilt Trail Coloring Book Two
Franklin County Vermont Barn Quilt Coloring Book

Geometric Patterns

Geometric Design Coloring Book 1
Geometric Design Coloring Book 2
Geometric Design Coloring Book 3
Geometric Design Coloring Book 4
Geometric Design Coloring Book 5

Graph Paper Designs

Create Geometric Quilt Designs with Graph Paper Designs

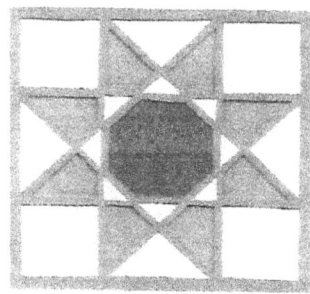 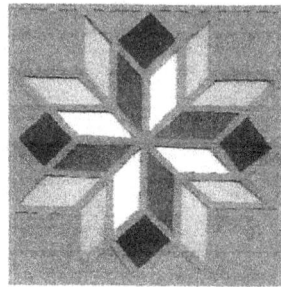 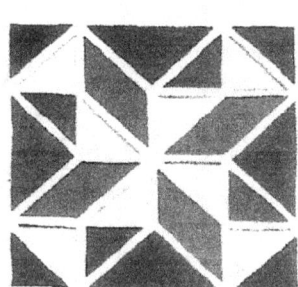

Coloring Relieves Stress and Tension
Order...John H. Lettau at Amazon.com

READING & MATH BOOKS by JOHN H. LETTAU

1st Dimension	Grades 3-6
2nd Dimension	Grades 3-6
Primary Dimension	Grades 1-4
Aztec Math Primary Book One	Grades 1-3
Aztec Math Primary Book Two	Grades 1-3
Aztec Math Intermediate Book One	Grades 3-6
Aztec Math Intermediate Book Two	Grades 3-6
Aztec Math Jr. High Book One	Grades 5-8
Aztec Math Jr. High Book Two	Grades 5-8
Aztec Math Decimal Book	Grades 4-8
Aztec Math Fraction Book	Grades 4-8
Sum-Action Number Puzzle Book One	Grades 3-6
Sum-Action Number Puzzle Book Two	Grades 3-6
Sum-Action Number Puzzle Primary Book One	Grades 1-3
Sum-Action Number Puzzle Primary Book Two	Grades 1-3
Multiplication Number Puzzles	Grades 3-6
Geometric Design Puzzle Book One	Grades 3-6
Geometric Design Puzzle Book Two	Grades 3-6
Aztec Reading Primary Book One	Grades 1-3
Aztec Reading Primary Book Two	Grades 1-3
Math in Action	Grades 3-6
A-Maze-ing Number Puzzles	Grades 3-6
Graph Paper Designs	Grades 2-6
Pick-A-Dilly Papers	Grades 3-6
Awards for All Reasons	Grades 1-6
Time Marches On	Grades 1-3
Pennies, Nickels & Dimes	Grades 1-3
Super-Sum Activity Cards	Grades 3-6
Learning Center Game Boards	Grades 1-3
Aztec Design Coloring Book	Grades 1-6

www.ingramcontent.com/pod-product-compliance
Lightning Source LLC
Chambersburg PA
CBHW060006230526
45472CB00008B/1967